"MY" Signature
"Gospel Birds'
(Fried Chicken Recipes)
and
Accompaniments
Cookbook

"MY" Signature "Gospel Birds' (Fried Chicken Recipes) and Accompaniments Cookbook

Sharon Hunt

Print information available on the last page.

Rev. date: 03/13/2019

To order additional copies of this book, contact:
Xlibris
1-888-795-4274
www.Xlibris.com
Orders@Xlibris.com
747920

About Sharon Hunt

Sharon Hunt, born in Nobletown and is a 1965 graduate of Wewoka High School. She graduated with B.S. and M.S Degrees from Oklahoma State University. She did further study at Kansas State University.

Ms. Hunt is a registered dietitian and worked as a dietitian at St. Luke's and Texas Children's Hospitals in Houston, Texas. Ms. Hunt taught food and nutrition for more than forty years at Langston University and Fort Valley State University, Fort Valley, Georgia. While at Fort Valley, Ms. Hunt wrote a cookbook Bread from Heaven and appeared on QVC Home Shopping Network three times. Ms. Hunt wrote the original recipe for the World Largest Peach Cobbler for Peach County, Georgia.

Ms. Hunt co-founded the undergraduate chapter of Delta Sigma Theta Sorority, Inc. at Oklahoma State University and served as the charter president of the Warner Robins Alumnae Chapter of Delta Sigma Theta Sorority, Inc. in Warner Robins, Georgia.

Currently, Ms. Hunt is retired from teaching and has begun a new career in African-American History. She has self-published 22 books on different aspects of history. She mainly writes about Oklahoma and Georgia.

She hopes to be on the move to write 11th grade Black history books and to include more history about the slaves in eleventh grade history in the United States.

CONTENTS

DEDICATION

Dedicated to Jesus Christ!

To all people who enjoy consuming the 'Gospel Bird'-

John 3:16

PREFACE

The purpose of "MY" Signature 'Gospel Birds' (Fried Chicken) and Accompaniments Cookbook is to show the slavery influences on gospel experiences and to illustrate how the preparation of recipes for fried chicken dinners varied in 14 states. The author has developed 14 different fried chicken recipes representing each of the fourteen states.

Also, included in each chapter are recipes for accompaniments and highlights popular in each state.

DISCLAIMER

All of the recipes for fried chicken and other recipes are developed by the author.

The idea is to highlight how fried chicken has been used at church meetings in the past.

INTRODUCTION

The 'Gospel Bird' is a nickname given to fried chicken as a popular entrée prepared and enjoyed at gospel events during plantation days by African-Americans as well as up to the present times. Fried chicken was prepared different by the Southern African -Americans in each state. It has been said that all slaves pride themselves in the varied recipes.

In this cookbook, "MY" Signature' Gospel Birds' (Fried Chicken Recipes) and Accompaniments Cookbook is designed to included my formulations of fried chicken and accompaniments recipes representing 14 states. Important highlights for each states and Bible scriptures also are included.

Each of the chapters will be outlined as follows: 'Gospel Bird' (Fried Chicken) and Accompaniments Menu, Recipes, Gospel Music and Musicians, Worship Meeting Places on the Plantations as told by former Slaves in the slave narratives, State Facts and Scriptures from the Bible.

'Gospel Birds'-What Makes Them Different?

For this cookbook, the Signature recipes in frying chicken are due to:
1. Seasoning Ingredients
2. Marinades and Marinating times
3. Methods of Battering
4. Frying Times and Utensils Used
5. Times of Frying

II. GOSPEL MUSIC AND MUSICIANS

The African-American song is said to have originated in Africa. African religion songs, lullabies and field hollers, songs in unison in call and response known as spirituals, once known as anthems.

PSALM 100

1. Make a joyful noise unto the Lord, all ye lands.
2. Serve the Lord with gladness; come before his presence with singing.
3. Know ye that the Lord he is God. It is he that hath made us and not we ourselves; we are his people, and the sheep of his pasture.
4. Enter into his gates with thanksgiving and into his courts with praise: be thankful unto him, and bless his name.
5. For the Lord is good, his mercy is everlasting: and his truth endureth to all genertions.

Slave songs heard on plantations from Virginia to Florida

1. A Little Talk with Jesus Makes It Right
2. Ah God's Chillun Got Wings
3. All I do, de Church Keep A-Grumblin'
4. By an'By
5. Chilly Waters
6. Come By Here, Lord!
7. Crucifixion
8. Daniel Saw di Stone
9. De Angel Roll de Stone Away
10. De Angel in Heab'n Gwineter Write My Name
11. Death Came to My House He Didn't Stay Long
12. De Band o' Gideon
13. De Angel in Heab'n Gwineter Write My Name

48. Walk in Jerusalem Jut like John
49. Walk Together Children
50. We are Climbin' Jacob's Ladder
51. Were You There When They Crucified My Lord?
52. Where Shall I Be When the Firs' Trumpet Sounds?
53. Where Was Peter?
54. Who Dat A-Comin' Ovah Yondah?
55. Who'll Be A Witness for My Lord?
56. You Go, I'll Go Wit You
57. You May Bury Me in De Eas'
58. You Mus' Hab Dat True Religion
59. Nobody Know de Trouble I See
60. O, Gambler, Git Up Off o' Yo Knees
61. O Wasn't Dat a Wide River?
62. Oh, Hear Me Prayin'
63. Peter, Go Ring Dem Bells
64. Ride On Moses
65. Roll, Jordan, Roll
66. Run, Mary, Run
67. Sinner, Please Don't Let dis Harvest Pass
68. Somebody's Knockin' at Yo' Dor'
69. Sometimes I Feel Like a Motherless Child
70. Stand Still Jordon
71. Steal Away to Jesus
72. Swing Low Sweet Chariot

Source: Johnson, James Weldon and J. Rosamond Johnson. The Books of American Negro Spirituals. Viking Press.

After-slavery, the ex-slaves were able to use musicals instruments in playing of music. The drums were used forbidden from use in slavery.

Gospel music and spirituals have been heard all throughout the plantations to South Carolina and Georgia.

The music antebellum and has a history in the Sea Islands are a chain of islands extending along coastal Georgia and South Carolina, from the mouth of the Santee River to the St. John River in Florida.

Slave music been heard all throughout the plantations in the South. The spirituals and anthems were heard more than 200 years ago.

Slaves would sing spirituals as they did their work, whether in the field or houses. Gospel music in Georgia was made popular in the Georgia Sea Islands, St. Simon's, Sapelo and Cumberland and Glynn County.

The main sea island that plantation songs were first recorded was St. Simon's Island. The wife of a slave owner organized musicals for the slaves from different plantations.

From that time, the same genre of music is incorporated in the Georgia Sea Island Festival held annually on

St. Simon's Island in August of each year. The Sea Island Festival is sponsored by the Glynn County Department of Leisure Services. There are many Sea Island Singers who participate. The purpose of the Festival is to present Sea Island music from Georgia, grape-vine crafts, Folk sculpture, Black smith art, row boat building, cotton and flax spinning, traditional arrow carving, crab traps making. Music include Sea Island music, slave songs and shouts, old-time choir singing, old-time spirituals, blues piano, guitar, banjo and buck dancing, old-time fiddler, work songs and shouts of slavery.

Some of the black families participating in the Georgia Sea Island Festival are said to trace their families heritage back to a spot in Africa in the town of Kianah in the District of Temourrah in the Kingdom of Messina which once was on the River Niger

IV. WORSHIP AND MEETING PLACES on the PLANTATION

During slavery, some slaves were prohibited from going to church. Others went to church with their owners and set at the back of the church or in the balconies of the white churches.

In this section, for each state selections are taken from the slave narratives to show how the slaves

Served the Lord. Also, the oldest AFRICAN -AMERICAN Baptist church after the Civil War will be highlighted.

After emancipation of slaves, the churches were used for educating the black children. At times, white teachers from the north would teach the children. The churches were named for places in the Bibles, Bible chapters or Jesus Christ.

VI. SCRIPTURE

New Testament

Matthew 6:24-34

24 No man can serve two masters for he will hate the one, and love the other, or else he will hold to the one
And despise the other. YE CANNOT SERVE GOD AND MAMMON.

25 Therefore I say unto you Take no thought for your life, what ye shall eat, what ye shall drink, and yet for your body what ye shall put on, is life more than meat, and the body then raiment?

26 Behold the fowls of the air: for they sow not, neither do they reap, nor gather into barns; yet your heavenly Father feedeth them. Are ye much better than they?

27 Which of you by taking thought can add one cubit unto his stature?

28 And why take ye thought for raiment? Consider the lilies of the field, how they grow; they toil not, neither do they spin.

29 And yet I say unto you, That even Solomon in all his glory, was not arrayed like one of these.

30 Wherefore, if God so clothe the grass of the field, which today is, and tomorrow is cast into the oven, shall he not much more clothe you, O ye of little faith.

31 Therefore take no thought saying what shall we eat? Or, What shall we Drink? Or Wherewithal shall we be clothed?

32 (For after all things do the Gentiles seek) For you Heavenly Father knoweth that ye have need of all these things.

33 But seek ye first the kingdom of God; and his righteousness; and all these things shall be added unto you.

34 Take therefore no thought for the morrow: for the morrow shall take thought for the things of itself. Sufficient unto the day is the evil thereof.

Chapter 1

ALABAMA

"MY" Signature Alabama 'Gospel Bird'(Fried Chicken) and Accompaniment Menu

-HIGHLIGHTS-

I. MENU

Signature 'Gospel Bird' (Fried Chicken)-Mustard Dipping Sauce
Alabama Collard Greens
Cornmeal Muffins
Plum Cobbler
Alabama Sweet Tea

II. RECIPES

"MY" SIGNATURE ALABAMA 'GOSPEL BIRD' (FRIED CHICKEN)

Amounts	Ingredients
1-3pound	fryer-cut-up
Brine:	
1 quart	water
½ cup	salt
¼ cup	apple cider vinegar
1 teaspoon	salt
1 ½ teaspoons	black pepper
1 teaspoon	paprika
½ teaspoon	cayenne pepper
½ teaspoon	salt
2 cups	buttermilk

2	eggs, beaten
3 cups	flour
2 cups s	hortening
1 cup	butter

Directions

1. Prepare chicken, place in a bowl cover and refrigerate until later.
2. Make brine -combine all brine ingredients in a saucepan and
3. Heat until salt has dissolved.
4. Cool brine and pour over chicken in the bowl cover with plastic wrap and refrigerated for 3 hours.
5. Remove chicken and rinse with cold water. Pat dry and then season, batter and fry.
6. In a small bowl, stir together seasoning ingredients.
7. Season chicken pieces.
8. In a bowl, beat eggs and buttermilk together.
9. Place flour in plastic bag.
10. Dip chicken piece by piece in buttermilk mixture.
11. Dip chicken piece by piece in a plastic bag of flour.
12. Refrigerate for ten minutes and then fry in hot fat.
13. Heat shortening and butter to 325 degrees F in large skillet.
14. Fry until golden brown on both sides.

MUSTARD DIPPING SAUCE RECIPE

Amounts	Ingredients
2 cups	prepared mustard
½ cup	cane syrup

Directions

1. Stir together all ingredients.
2. Serve.

ACCOMPANIMENTS

ALABAMA COLLARD GREENS

Amounts	Ingredients
¼ pound	ham hocks, cured
2 quarts	water
2 bunches	collards, chopped
1 pound	cabbage, chopped
½ teaspoon	red pepper flakes
11/2 teaspoons	salt

Directions

1. Clean ham hocks.
2. Place in a large boiling saucepot with water. Boil until tender. Remove meat from water and chop.
3. Wash collard greens, roll up leaves and chop. Stir collard greens and red pepper flakes into large saucepot with water.
4. Bring to boil and then turn to medium low and cook for 1 hour Stirring occasionally.
5. Stir in chopped cabbage and cooked ham hock. Stir in salt. Cover and cook for 15 minutes or until desired doneness.

CORNMEAL MUFFINS

Amount	Ingredients
2 cups	corn meal, white
½ cup	flour
2 tablespoons	baking powder
1 teaspoon	salt
1 teaspoon	baking soda
3 tablespoons	sugar
1 ¼ cups	buttermilk

| 2 | eggs, slight beaten |
| 3 tablespoons | lard, melted |

Directions

1. Preheat oven to 400 degrees F. Melt 1 tablespoons shortening in microwave and coat each cup in muffin pan.
2. Set aside.
3. In a large bowl, stir together all dry ingredients. Set aside.
4. Whip together liquid ingredients and stir into dry ingredients.
5. Pour into muffin cups and bake for 15 minutes or until done.
6. Serve hot.

PLUM COBBLER

Amount	Ingredients
Topping	
2 cups	all-purpose flour
1 cups	sugar
1 cup	brown sugar
1 cup	butter
1 teaspoon	salt
Filling	
3 pounds	plums, sliced
½ cup	water
2 tablespoons	lemon juice
½ teaspoon	salt
1 ½ cups	sugar
2 tablespoons	cornstarch
½ teaspoon	cinnamon
1/ teaspoon	ginger

Directions

1. In a large bowl, combine the topping ingredients to the size of small peas. Set aside.
2. In a medium size sauce pan, combine plums, water, lemon juice and salt. Cook for minutes.
3. Stir in sugar, cornstarch and spices. Cook for 10 minutes until thicken.
4. Cool and pour into 13 x 9 x 2 -inch pan. Sprinkle top with topping and bake for 45 minutes or until golden brown.
5. Serve: 10-15 -1/2 cups servings.

ALABAMA SWEET TEA

Amount	Ingredients
3 family-size	tea bags
1 gallon	hot water
1 cup	honey
1 cup	sugar
2	lemons, sliced

Direction

1. Steep the tea in the boiling water. Cool down.
2. Stir honey and sugar into tea until dissolved.
3. Serve with sliced lemons.

-HIGHLIGHTS-

III. GOSPEL MUSIC AND MUSICIANS

1. Sources of Gospel musicians and their born in Alabama
    Singer   Hometown
1. Inez Andrews   Birmingham
    Sinner's Prayer
2. The Alabama Boys

Songs-Never Alone, Prayer is the Key, Stay on the Water, Jesus You, Bought Me, He Kept Me

3. The 5 Blind Boys of Alabama Talladega
   Songs-Draw Me Nearer, I'm Not that Way Anymore

4. Gospel Harmoneeres - Birmingham
   Songs- Lift Him Up
   Never Grow Old
   3. Ministers on Record Born in Alabama
   -Rev. B.W. Smith- born in Florence Alabama

List on recorded sermons

1. Faith Tried by Fire
2. Hands of God
3. Watch Them Dogs and Roots
4. Run and Tell That and All King's Men
5. The Bones in the Valley.

III. WORSHIP MEETINGS PLACES ON THE PLANTATION

(One Ex-Slave's Account from the Alabama Slave Narratives)

"O yessum, I used to go to meetin'. Us niggers didn't have no meetin' house on de plantation, but Marse Jim 'lowed us to build a bresh arbor.

Den two years atter de surrender took consideration and j'ined in wid de Lawd. Dat's how come I live so long. De Lawd done told me. 'Antn'y, you got a hundred and twenty miles to trabel. Dat mean got gwine to live a hundred abd twenty years if you stay on de straight and narrow road.

But if you don't, you gotter go jes' de same as all de yuther's."

"Tell me something about your master's slaves and overseers.' I asked him. "Well" he said, "Marse Jim had 'bout three hundred slaves and he had one mighty bad overseer."

Ex-Slave Anthony Crombley, Alabama

Camp Meeting

"Saturday nights they could sing and dance and have prayer meetings, then on some Sundays, they could hitch up the mules to a big wagon and all go to the white folks church; and again there would be camp meetings held and the slaves from all the surrounding plantations would attend going to same."

"These large wagons sometimes having four mules to a wagon. They would have a good time along the way, singing and calling to one another and making friends."

Ex-Slave Charles Aarons
Oak Grove, Alabama

-OLDEST BLACK BAPTIST CHURCH IN

ALABAMA

-St. Bartley Primitive Baptist Church in Huntsville, Alabama established in 1808. The church was formed by enslaved people for Georgia bought to Alabama.

V. ALABAMA STATE FACTS

Alabama -The Yellowhammer State
        -The Heart of Dixie

Admission to the Union -December 14, 1819

Slave State -1819-1865(Alabama served as part of the Confederacy from 1861 to 1865. South Carolina seceded first from the Union. The states that followed South Carolina were Mississippi, Florida, Georgia, Louisiana, Texas, Virginia, Arkansas,
Tennessee and North Carolina.)
Named after a tribe of Creek Indians Nation
Motto: Audemus jura nostra defendere-We dare to defend our rights
State Song: Alabama
State Flower -Camellia
State Bird -Yellowhammer
State Tree – Longleaf Pine
Capital City: Montgomery
Largest City- Birmingham
Oldest City: Mobile
Location: Located in the southeastern region in the United States.
Bordered in the north by Tennessee;
In the east by Georgia;
In the south Florida and the Gulf of Mexico;
In the west- Mississippi
Number of Counties in Alabama-67 counties –
Alabama ranks number 3 in the production of poultry. Chicken producers in 35 counties.

VI. SCRIPTURES

EXODUS 8:1

And the Lord spake unto Moses. Go unto Pharaoh, and say unto him, Thus saith the Lord, Let my people go, that they may serve me.

Chapter 2

ARKANSAS

"MY" Signature Arkansas 'Gospel Bird' (Fried Chicken) and Accompaniments Menu

-HIGHLIGHTS-

I. MENU

"MY" Signature Arkansas 'Gospel Bird' (Fried Chicken)
Collard Greens and Kale
Corn Bread
Green Apple Cobbler
"MY" Arkansas-Style Lemon Iced Tea

II. RECIPES

"MY" Signature Arkansas 'Gospel Bird'(Fried Chicken)

Amounts	Ingredients
2 pounds	fryer, cut up
2 teaspoons	black pepper
1 ½ teaspoons	salt
1 cup	ice water
2	eggs, beaten
3 tablespoons	cornstarch
2 cups	flour
	Oil for frying

Directions

1. Cut-up and wash chicken. Pat dry. Season with salt and pepper. Set aside.

2. In a bowl, combine water and egg and beat well. Add cornstarch and flour. Stir well and well blended.
3. Carefully coat each piece of chicken with mixture. Refrigerate for 30 minutes.
4. Heat oil to 375 degrees F. for frying in a heavy skillet.
5. Fry chicken until golden brown. Drain on paper towels. Serve hot.

Dipping Sauce

Amounts	Ingredients
1 cup	ketchup
½ cup	hot sauce
¼ cup	brown sugar
¼ cup	apple cider vinegar

Directions

1. Stir well and heat in microwave for 2 minutes.
2. Cool and serve with chicken.

ACCOMPANIMENTS

Collard Greens/Kale

Amounts	Ingredients
1 pound	salt pork, cut up
2 quarts	water
2 bunches	collard greens, Cut up
1 bunch	kale, cut up
2 teaspoons	salt
1 tablespoon	sugar
2 tablespoons	lard
½ tablespoon	red pepper flakes

Directions

1. In large stockpot, boil salt pork in water until done.
2. Stir in greens and continue to cook. Add 1 cup of boiling water.
3. Stir well. Add remaining ingredients. Cover and cook on low for 1 ½ hours or until done.

Cornbread

Amounts	Ingredients
2 cups	stone- ground cornmeal
1 cup	flour
½ teaspoon	soda
11/2 teaspoons	baking powder
1 teaspoon	salt
½ cup	sugar
11/4 cups	buttermilk
2	eggs, beaten

Directions

1. Heat oven to 400 degrees F. Grease baking pan with shortening.
2. Sift together all dry ingredients.
3. Add buttermilk and beaten eggs.
4. Stir until dry ingredients are mixed.
5. Pour into the baking pan.
6. Bake for 15 minutes or until golden brown.

Green Apple Cobbler

Amounts	Ingredients
3 pounds	Granny Smith Apples, peel and sliced
1	water

2 tablespoons	cornstarch
2 tablespoons	lemon juice
1 cup	butter, chopped
2 cups	sugar
¾ cup	brown sugar
1 teaspoon	salt
1 teaspoon	cinnamon
2	prepared pastry for 13 x 9x 2 -inch for top and bottom

Directions

1. Peel, core and slice apples and place in large pan. Add water. Cook on low for 5 minutes. Gradually add cornstarch, lemon juice, butter, sugars, salt and cinnamon. Toss well.
2. Cook on low until sugar is dissolved.
3. Cool filling. Arrange bottom crust in a large 13 x 9x 2 -inch baking pan. Prick with fork.
4. Arrange apple filling in pan on top of bottom crust.
5. Cover with top pastry. Prick crust with a fork.
6. Bake for 25-30 minutes on until desired doneness.

"MY" Arkansas-Style Lemon Iced Tea

Amount	Ingredients
2	family-sized tea bags
1 gallon	water
2 cups	sugar
1 can	lemonade

Directions

1. In a large stockpot, boil water and tea bags together for 5 minutes. Remove tea bags and dissolve sugar. Cool.
2. Stir in lemonade.

-HIGHLIGHTS-

III. GOSPEL MUSIC AND MUSICIANS

Roberta Martin Singers-Helena, Arkansas

1. God Specializes
2. He Has Done Great Things For Me
3. Walk on By Faith
4. There is no Failure in God
5. No Other Help I Know
6. I'm Glad I'm A Witness for MY God

Sister Rosetta Tharpe – Cotton Plant, Arkansas

1- Precious Memories
2- No Room in the Cherish for Liars
3- Saviour Don't Pass Me By
4- Walking Up the King's Highway
5- Precious Lord Take My Hand

IV. WORSHIP MEETING PLACES ON THE PLANTATIONS

Going to the White Church

"On dem Sundays dat de marster sent all de niggers ter go ter church fer de preachin'; he send dem all de order wush up good an clean an put ter be gwine on ter de church an dey go on as in sit in de bak

13

behind all preach. Dar wasn't no nigger preachers in dem days dat I ever seed."

Ex-Slave Henry Bartain, Arkansas

Vol2, Part 3-Page 95

Church in the Quarters

"I was born three miles west of Starkville, Mississippi on pretty tolerable large farm. My folks was bought from a speculator drove come by. They come from Sanders in South Ca'lina. Master Charlie Cannon bought a whole drove of us, both my grandparents on both sides. He had five farms. Saturday was ration day.

"I never went to school in my life.

I was taught by the preacher to be obedient and not steal.

"We et outer trays hewed out of logs. Three of us would eat together. We had wooden spoons. The boys made whittling about in cold rainy weather. We all hav gourds to drink outer. When we had milk

We'd get on our knees and turn up the tray. Same way wid pot-liquor. They give the grown up the meat and us pot liquor."

Ex-Slave Frank Cannon

Palestine, Arkansas, age 77

OLDEST BLACK BAPTIST CHURCH IN ARKANSAS

First Missionary Baptist Church in Little Rock in the oldest black church. Founded in 1845 by a slave master named Reverend Wilson Brown.

V. ARKANSAS STATE FACTS

Arkansas-The Natural State
Capital City-Little Rock
Number of Counties -77 counties
Admitted to the Union-June 15, 1836 (25th State)
Slave State from 1836 to 1865.
Named derived from an Osage Indian language
Border States:
North- Missouri
East-Tennessee
Southeast -Mississippi
South-Louisiana
Southwest-Texas
West _Oklahoma

VI. SCRIPTURES FROM THE BIBLE

OLD TESTAMENT

DEUTERONOMY2:7

7For the Lord thy God hath blessed thee in all the works of thy hand: he knoweth thy walking through this great wilderness: these forty years The Lord thy God hath been with thee; thou hast lacked nothing.
Deuteronomy 2:7

CHAPTER 3

FLORIDA

"MY" Signature Florida 'Gospel Bird' (Fried Chicken) and Accompaniments Menu

-HIGHLIGHTS-

I. MENU

Mango Dipping Sauce
Florida Greens
Corn bread
"MY" Florida Mango/ Peach Cobbler
Florida Sweet Tea

II. RECIPES

"MY" Signature Florida 'Gospel Bird' (Fried Chicken)

Amount	Ingredients
3 pound	fryer, cutup
3	limes
1 ½ teaspoons	seasoned salt
1 teaspoon	black pepper
1 teaspoon	garlic granules
3 cups	self-rising flour
4 cups	peanut oil

Directions

1. Clean and wash chicken.
2. Place in a bowl and squeeze lime juice over each piece of chicken. Refrigerated covered for 2 hours.

3. In a small bowl, stir.
4. together all seasoning and set aside.
5. Remove chicken from refrigerator, wash and pat dry.
6. Season with seasoning.
7. Roll in flour.
8. Fry until golden brown in hot peanut oil(350 degrees F).

Mango Dipping Sauce

Amount	Ingredients
2 cups	mango, cubed
1 cup	sugar
1 ½ cups	water
¼ cup	hot sauce

Directions

1. Boil mango and sugar in water until mango is tender.
2. Place in food processor.
3. Add hot sauce and salt.
4. Cook for 5 minutes or until thick.

ACCOMPANIMENTS

Florida Greens

Amounts	Ingredients
1 gallon	water
1 bunch	collard greens, chopped
1	ham hock, chopped
1 teaspoon	red pepper flakes
¼ cup	canola oil
2 cloves	garlic, minced
1 tablespoon	salt

Directions

1. Using a large stock pot, bring water to boil and then stir in c Hopped greens.
2. Add ham hocks, red pepper flakes and canola oil.
3. Cover and cook over medium heat for 2 hours. Add water if needed.
4. Stir in remaining ingredients. Cover and cook for an additional 30 minutes.

Corn Bread

Amount	Ingredients
2 cups	yellow corn meal
¼ cup	flour
1 teaspoon	baking powder
2 tablespoons	sugar
1 teaspoon	salt
1 cup	whole kernel corn
1	cup milk
1	egg, beaten
½ cup	butter melted

Directions

1. In a bowl combine all dry ingredients.
2. Stir in corn. Stir in milk, egg and butter.
3. Pour into prepared pan and bake for 10 minutes until golden brown.

"MY" Florida Mango/Peach Cobbler

Amount	Ingredients
1	crust to fit top and bottom of 13 x 9 x 2 -inch cobbler pan

2 cups	mango, sliced in 1 inch long slices
1 cup	peaches, sliced
½ cup	sugar
¾ cup	brown sugar
¼ cup	flour
1 cup	water
1 teaspoon	cinnamon
1 teaspoon	salt
1 tablespoon	lemon juice
½ teaspoon	almond extract
¼ cup	butter, melted

Directions

1. Preheat oven to 400 degrees. F. Place one crust in bottom of 13 x 9 x 2 -inch pan and prick with a fork.
2. Bake bottom crust for 5 minutes remove from oven and cool.
3. Prepare mango and peach slices. Stir together and set aside.
4. In a medium sauce pan, stir together sugar, brown sugar, flour and water.
5. Bring to a slow boil and cook until thickens.
6. Stir together all ingredients and arrange on top of bottom cobbler crust.
7. Place top crust over mixture. Prick holes in top with a fork.
8. Bake at 350 degrees F. for 35 minutes.

Florida Sweet Tea

Amount	Ingredients
1 family size	tea bag
1 gallon	water
2 cups	sugar
2 cups	orange juice
1 cup	lemon juice

| 1 cup | mango juice |
| ¼ cup | lime juice |

Directions

1. Boil water and steep tea. Remove tea bag and stir in sugar.
2. Cool down and stir in remaining ingredients.

II.   GOSPEL MUSIC AND MUSICIANS

1.   The Consolers -Husband/Wife

Songs

1. Give God Thanks
2. Getting Ready For the Rapture
3. Waiting for my Child to Come Home
4. Christ Makes the Difference
5. Jordan River
6. I Feel Good
7. Oh How Happy I Will Be

2.   Tommy Ellison- Plant City

Songs

1. Let this Be a Lesson to You

3.   Florida Mass Choir

Songs

1. Let the Holy Ghost Lead You
2. The Lord Will Make Away Somehow
3. I Made it Over

4. Troy Sneed – Jacksonville

Songs

1. Call Jesus
2. Let's Praise Him
3. Walk Around Heaven
4. He's Sweet
5. The Lord on Your Side

IV. WORSHIP MEETINGS PLACES ON THE PLANTATIONS

Church on the Plantation in Florida

"He states that he enjoyed his slavery life and since that time

His life has been sweet. He knows and remembers most of the incidents with members of the several conferences of the African Methodist Episcopal Churches in Florida and can tell you in what minutes you may find many any of the important happenings of the past 30 or 40 years."

Personal Interviews with Samuel Simeon Andrews Edwards; Edward Waters College, Kings Road, Jacksonville, Florida

Samuel Simeon Andrews
Jacksonville, Florida

OLDEST BLACK BAPTIST CHURCH IN FLORIDA

-Bethel Baptist Institutional Church of Jacksonville has been recognized as the oldest Black Baptist church in Florida. The church was established on a plantation in the 1830s.

V. STATE FACTS

Florida -Admitted to the Union in 1845.

State Nickname -Sunshine State

Florida history- The Spanish explorers Juan Ponce de Leon in 1513 made the first visits.

Spanish conquered the land of Florida later on. In 1920s, Florida had highest amounts of lynchings and black massacres.

Capital City of Florida – Tallahassee
State Flower -Orange Blossom
State Animal – Florida Panther
State Beverage -Orange juice
State Bird – Mockingbird
State Butterfly Zebra Longwing
State Day – April 2-
State Flower Orange Blossom
State Gem – Moonstone
State Reptile -Alligator
State Song – The Suwanee River
State Tree- Sabal Palm
Florida has more than 25 poultry processing plants.

VI. SCRIPTURES IN THE BIBLE

PSALM 19:14

14 Let the words of my mouth and the meditation of my heart, be acceptable in thy sight, O Lord,
My strength and my redeemer.

PSALM 19:14

CHAPTER 4

GEORGIA

"MY" Signature Georgia 'Gospel Bird' (Fried
Chicken) and Accompaniments Menu

-HIGHLIGHTS-

I. MENU

"MY" Signature Georgia 'Gospel Bird'(Fried Chicken) Menu
Georgia Popular Dipping Sauce
Macaroni and Cheese
Sweet Potato Souffle
Georgia Collard Greens
Potato Salad
Corn Bread Patties
Peach Cobbler
Georgia Sweet Tea

Georgia Popular Dipping Sauce

Amount	Ingredients
½ cup	hot sauce
¼ cup	Tabasco sauce
1/ 2 cup	apple cider vinegar
1/4 teaspoon	salt

Directions

1. Place all ingredients in a large jar. Shake well.
2. Serve.

II. RECIPES

"MY" Signature Georgia 'Gospel Bird' (Fried Chicken) Recipe

Amounts	Ingredients
21/2 -3 pound	fryer, cut-up
3 cups	buttermilk
1 tablespoon	apple cider vinegar
2 ½ cups	flour
1 teaspoon	salt
1 ¾ teaspoons	black pepper
1 teaspoon	paprika
1 teaspoon	garlic salt
11/2 teaspoons	onion powder
4 ups	peanut oil or vegetable oil

For frying

Directions

1. Clean and wash chicken. Set aside. In a large bowl combine buttermilk and apple cider vinegar. Stir well. Place chicken pieces in mixture; cover all pieces. Wrap bowl in plastic wrap. Refrigerate for 3 hours.
2. In a large plastic container, combine flour, salt, black pepper, paprika, garlic salt and onion powder. Stir well. Remove chicken from refrigerator.
3. Heat oil in a large skillet.
4. Dip chicken pieces one by one in flour mixture.
5. Place large pieces in skillet first and fry to golden brown on both sides.
6. Drain and serve hot.

ACCOMPANIMENTS

Macaroni and Cheese

Amount	Ingredients
1-box	macaroni elbow noodles
½ cup	onions, chopped
1 tablespoon	butter
1 tablespoon	flour.
1 cup	milk
1 cup	sharp cheddar cheese, grated
½ cup	medium cheddar cheese, grated
1	egg, slightly beaten
1 teaspoon	salt
1 cup	mild cheddar cheese for topping

Directions

1. Prepare macaroni as stated on the package. Drain. Set aside.
2. Butter 3 quart casserole dish. Set aside.
3. Prepare onion and cook in a saucepan with butter until tender.
4. Stir in flour, Gradually add milk. Stirring constantly.
5. Place in a large bowl, stir in cheeses. Cool down. Stir in egg. Stir in salt
6. Whip in macaroni noodles. Pour into casserole dish.
7. Top with mild cheddar cheese.
8. Bake at 350 degrees F. until golden brown.

Sweet Potato Souffle

Amount	Ingredients
2 ponds	sweet potatoes
1 cup	sugar
½ cup	brown sugar

½ teaspoon	cinnamon
1 cup	butter
2	eggs, slightly beaten
1 teaspoon	salt
1 cup	evaporated milk

Directions

1. Peel and cut up sweet potatoes. Wash and place in medium-sized saucepan. Cover with water and cook until soft. Drain and mash.
2. In a large bowl, place mashed sweet potatoes and beat in remaining ingredients.
3. Pour into a buttered 2 -quart casserole dish.
4. Bake at 350 degrees F. until done.

ACCOMPANIMENTS

Georgia Collard Greens

Amount	Ingredients
½ pound	cured neckbones
1 quart	water
2 bunches	collard greens, washed, stems removed and chopped
½ cup	onion, chopped
2 tablespoons	shortening
½ teaspoon	red pepper flakes
1 ½ teaspoons	salt

Directions

1. Wash and clean cured neckbones.
2. Place water in a large stockpot; add cured neckbones and boil covered until tender.

3. Stir in collard greens, onion and shortening. Cover and cook 30 minutes.
4. Stir in red pepper flakes and salt. Cover and continue to cook on medium heat until desired doneness.

Potato Salad

Amount	Ingredients
2 pounds	white potatoes, diced
3 large	eggs, hard-boiled chopped
1 cup	mayonnaise
¼ cup	onions, minced
½ cup	sweet pickle cubes
¼ cup	pimento, chopped
¼ cup	mustard
1 teaspoon	salt
1 teaspoon	paprika
½ teaspoon	cracked black pepper

Directions

1. Boil potatoes and eggs until tender. Eggs should be hard boiled.
2. Combine drained potatoes, chopped eggs and remaining ingredients in a large bowl.
3. Place in a covered bowl and refrigerate for 3 hours.

Corn Bread Patties

Amount	Ingredients
3 cups	corn meal
½ cup	flour
2 teaspoons	salt
1 teaspoon	baking powder

1	egg, lightly beaten
1 ½ cups	milk
1 cup	oil for frying

Directions

1. In a bowl, combine corn meal, flour, salt and baking powder, stir well. Set aside.
2. Combine egg and milk. Stir in the meal mixture.
3. In a skillet, heat up oil.
4. Fry ¼ cup batter per patty. Drain on paper towel. Should make 10 patties.

Peach Cobbler

Amount	Ingredients
2	prepared crusts for 13 x9x 2 inch pan
3 pounds	peaches, slices
1 cup	sugar
¾ cup	brown sugar
½ cup	self-rising flour
1 teaspoon	cinnamon
1 teaspoon	salt
1 teaspoon	lemon juice
1 cup	evaporated milk

Directions

1. Place one of the crusts in bottom of a 13 x 9 x 2 =inch pan. Prick bottom and Bake for 5 minutes.
2. In a bowl mix peaches with remaining ingredients.
3. Spread mixture over cooled crust and then spread second crust over top. Prick the top and then bake at 350 degrees F. or until done.

Georgia Sweet Tea

Amounts	Ingredients
2 family-sized	tea bags
1 gallon	water
2 cups	Dixie Crystal sugar

Directions

1. Boil tea bags in water.
2. Stir in sugar.
3. Remove tea bags.
4. Cool. Serve.

-HIGHLIGHTS-

III. GOSPEL MUSIC AND MUSICIANS

Singer Birthplace

1.   Thomas A. Dorsey Villa Rica

Considered the Father of Gospel Music.

Songs

1. Take My Hand, Precious Lord
2. It's A Highway to Heaven
3. Hid Me in thy Bosom
4. I'm Going to Live the Life I Sing About!
5. Peace in the Valley
6. I Don't Know Why
7. The Lord Will Make A Way Some how
8. Old Ship of Zion

2.   Singers

The Anointed Pace Sisters Atlanta

1.   Praise the Lord
2.   To Be Like Jesus
3.   My Purpose

LaShon Pace Rhodes Atlanta

Songs

1.   He Lives

3.   SheKinah Glory

4.   The Suwanee Quintet Augusta

Songs

q. Just One Rose Will Do
Ministers

The Rev. Timothy Flemings Macon

Famous Sermons

1.   What Jealousy Will Do!
2.   Too Close Too Heaven

Minister

Rev. Benjamin Cove Jr

1.   Birds in the Church
2.   The House is Open

3. Sketches of My Life
4. Prayer for AmerIca

III. WORSHIP MEETING PLACES ON THE PLANTATION

"Meeting Day"

"Some slaves larnt to read and write. If dey went to meetin' dey had to go wid deir white folks 'cause dey didn't have to sep'rate churches fer de Niggers 'till atter de war. On our Marster's place, slaves didn't go off to meetin' t'all. Sey jus' went 'round to one anothers houses and sing songs. Some of 'em 'read de Bible by heart. Once I heared a man preach what didn't know how to read one word in de Bible and he didn't been have no Bible yet.

"De first baptizin' I ever was atter I was nigh bout grown. If a slave from our place ever jined up wid a church 'fore de war was over. I never heered tell nothin' 'bout it.

"Lordy, Miss! I didn't know nothin' 'bout what funeral was dem days. If a nigger died des mornin' dey sho' didn't want no time a-puttin' him right on down in de ground dat same day. Dem coffins' never had no shape to 'em dey was jus square."

Ex-Slave Rachel Adams, Age 78 years
Georgia,

OLDEST BLACK BAPTIST CHURCH IN GEORGIA

The oldest black Baptist church is located in Savannah -First African Baptist Church formed in 1773.

IV.   STATE FACTS

Georgia -4th State of U.S.
Georgia State Capital -Atlanta
State Nickname – the Peach State
State Motto –"Wisdom, Justice and Moderation"
State Fruit_ Peach
State Food -Grits
State Vegetable- Vidalia Onion
State Crop – Peanut
State Song- 'Georgia on My Mind'

Number of Counties -159
State Flower – Cherokee Rose
State Tree- Live Oak
State Bird- Brown Thrasher
State Butterfly -Tiger Swallowtail
State Fish -Largemouth Bass
State Insect -Honey Bee
State Fossil -Shark Tooth
State Reptile -Gopher Tortoise
State Amphibian -Green Tree Frog
State Dance -Square Dancing
State Mineral - Staurolite

Number of Travel Regions

1. Presidential Pathways
2. Plantation Trace
3. Colonial Georgia
4. Historic Heartland
5. Northeast Georgia Mountains
6. Historic High Country
7. Atlanta Metro
8. Classic South

9. Plantation Trace
10. Magnolia Midlands
11. Georgia Coast

V.   SCRIPTURE from the BIBLE

JOSHUA 1:9

Have I not commanded you!
Be strong and of good courage
Do not be afraid, nor be dismayed
For the LORD, your God is with you
Wherever you go!

Joshua 1:9

CHAPTER 5

KENTUCKY

"MY" Signature Kentucky 'Gospel Bird' (Fried Chicken) and Accompaniments Menu

-HIGHLIGHTS-

I. MENU

"MY" Signature Kentucky 'Gospel Bird' (Fried Chicken)
Teriyaki Dipping Sauce
Stewed Collard Greens
Cornbread Muffins
Cantaloupe Gobbler
Peppermint Sweet Tea

II. RECIPES

"MY" Signature Kentucky 'Gospel Bird' (Fried Chicken) Recipe

Amounts	Ingredients
3 pounds	fryer, cut -up
marinade	
2 cups	vinegar
½ cup	olive oil
1/ teaspoon	basil
½ teaspoon	rosemary
2/3 tablespoon	salt
1 tablespoon	white pepper
1 ½ teaspoons	black pepper

1 tablespoon	celery salt
1 teaspoon	mustard, dry
2 teaspoons	garlic salt
1 teaspoon	oregano
½ tablespoons	thyme
¾ cup	flour
1 cup	milk
1	egg, well beaten
¾ cup	flour
3 cups	oil for deep-fat frying

Directions

1. Wash and cut up chicken. Set aside.
2. In a bowl, combine the ingredients for the marinade. Coat the cut-up chicken cover and refrigerate for three hours. Wash chicken and pat dry.
3. In a large bowl, combine salt, white pepper, black pepper, celery salt, mustard, garlic salt, oregano and thyme. Stir well. Season chicken.
4. Dredge in the first ¾ cup of flour. Dust excess flour from chicken. Set aside.
5. Mix together egg and milk in a bowl. Stir well.
6. Dip chicken in mixture.. Drain. Dredge into second ¾ cup of flour.
7. Deep fat fry in hot oil until done.

Teriyaki Dipping Sauce

Amount	Ingredients
½ cup	soy sauce
1 clove	garlic, minced
½ cup	sugar

2 tablespoons	Worcestershire sauce
½ teaspoon	salt
1 cup	pineapple juice

Directions
1. Combine all ingredients in a medium sauce pan.
2. Brin to a boil for 2 minutes then cook on medium for 10 minutes.
3. Remove garlic and serve.

ACCOMPANIMENTS

Stewed Collard Greens

Amount	Ingredients
2	oxtails
1	cured pig tail, chopped
3 cups	water
2 bunches	collard greens, washed and cut-up
1 medium	yellow onion, diced
1 ½ teaspoons	salt
½ teaspoon	red pepper flakes
2 tablespoons	lard

Directions
1. Wash and chop collard greens. Set aside.
2. In a large saucepan, combine meats and water. Cover and cook on medium heat for 40 minutes.
3. Stir in collard greens and diced onions. Bring to a boil for 5 minutes and then cook on medium low for 10 minute; add salt, red pepper flakes and lard. Stir well. Cook on medium low for 30 minutes or until desired doneness.

Cornbread Muffins

Amount	Ingredients
1 cup	corn meal
1 cup	all purpose flour
¼ cup	sugar
2 ½ teaspoons	baking powder
1 cup	buttermilk
½ cup	butter, melted
1	egg, slightly beaten
½ cup	white onion, minced
¼ cup	bell pepper, minced
¼ cup	red bell pepper, minced

Directions

1. Preheat oven to 400 degrees F. Grease 12 cup muffin pan. Set aside.
2. In a large bowl, stir together corn meal, all purpose flour, sugar and baking powder.
3. In a bowl, stir together buttermilk, butter and egg. Pour in the middle of dry ingredients.
4. Fold in onion and peppers.
5. Fill muffin cups to ¾ cup.
6. Bake for 15-20 minutes or until done.

Cantaloupe Cobbler

Amount	Ingredients
3	phyllo crusts to fit 13 x 9 x 2-inch pan
½ cup	butter, melted
4 cups	cantaloupe slices, 2-inch x 1 inch

1 cup	evaporated milk
1 teaspoon	cinnamon
¾ cup	sugar
½ teaspoon	salt
1 cup	water
1 tablespoon	lemon juice
½ teaspoon	almond extract

Topping

Amount	ingredients
1 cup	butter, melted
¼ cup	sugar
½ teaspoon	cinnamon

Directions

1. Separate phyllo crusts. Brush each with melted butter. Arrange one crust on the bottom of a 13 x 9 x 2 -inch pan.
2. Prepare cantaloupe slices. Set aside.
3. In a saucepan, stir together evaporated milk, cinnamon, sugar, salt and water.
4. Dissolve on low heat. Cool down.
5. Combine cantaloupe slices, milk mixture, lemon juice and almond extract. Toss together.
6. Arrange ½ of the mixture on top of the bottom crust.
7. Place second crust on top of the mixture.
8. Spoon remaining cantaloupe mixture on the middle crust. Spread evenly.
9. Place third crust on top. Prick top with fork.. Set aside.
10. Make topping. In a small bowl, stir together butter, sugar and cinnamon.
11. Thinly spread topping on crust.
12. Bake cobbler for30 minutes at 350 degrees F.

Peppermint Sweet Tea

Amount	Ingredients
1 gallon	water
1 family -size	tea bag
1 cup	peppermint candy, crushed
1 cup	sugar

Directions
1. In a large saucepot, boil water. Then steep tea bag for `0 minutes.
2. Dissolve peppermint candy and sugar in hot tea.
3. Serve over ice,

-HIGHLIGHTS-

III. GOSPEL MUSIC AND MUSICIANS

NOT KNOWN

IV. WORSHIP MEETING PLACES ON THE PLANTATIONS

'Church on the Plantation'

"I saw the slaves in chains after they were sold. The white folks did not teach us to read and write.

We had church on the plantation but we went from plantation to another to hear the preaching. White folks preacher name mins Reuben Lee, in Versailles. A meeting of the Baptist Church results in the first baptizing I ever saw. It was Mr. Chillers pond. The preachers would say 'I am baptizing you in Mr. Chillers pond because I know he is an honest man."

Ex-Slave George Henderson, Kentucky
Garrard County

Oldest Black Baptist Church in Kentucky

-First African Baptist Church in Lexington. The church was built in 1856.

V. STATE FACTS

Kentucky
State Capital – Frankfort
Largest City- Louisville

37th biggest state

Border States – Illinois, Indiana, Missouri, Ohio, Tennessee, Virginia and West Virginia.

Birthplace of Abraham Lincoln
Born in Kentucky, February 1, 1809
16th president of United States

VI. SCRIPTURES FROM THE BIBLE

PSALM 27

1. The Lord is my light and my salvation, whom shall I fear? The Lord is the strength of my life, of whom shall I be afraid?
2. When t he wicked, even mine enemies and my foes, came upon me to eat my flesh, they stumble and fall.
3. Though an host should encamp against me, my heart shall not fear:
    Though war shall rise against me, in this will I be confident.
4. One thing have I desired of the Lord, that will I seek after, that I may dwell in the house of the Lord all the days of my life, to behold the beauty of the Lord, and to inquire of his people.

5. For in the time of trouble he shall hide me in his pavilion: in the secret of his tabernacle shall be
Hide me; he shall set me upon a rock.

6. And now shall mine head be lifted up above mine enemies round above me: therefore, will I offer in his tabernacles sacrifices of joy: I will sing, yea, I will sing praises unto the Lord.

7. Hear, O Lord, when I cry with my voice: have mercy upon me, and answer me.

8. When, thou saidst, seek ye my face; my heart said unto me, Thy face, Lord, will I seek.

9. Hide not thy face far from me, put not thy servant away in anger: thou hast been my help; leave me not, neither forsake me, O God of my salvation.

10. When my father and my mother forsake me, then the Lord will take me up.

11. Teach me thy way, O Lord and lead me in a plain path, because of mine enemies.

12. Deliver me not over unto the will of mine enemies for false witnesses are risen up against me
And such as breathe and cruelty.

13. I had fainted unless I had believed to see the goodness of the Lord in the land of the living.

14. Wait on the Lord: be of good courage, and he s hall strengthen thine heart, wait, I say, on the Lord.

CHAPTER 6

LOUISIANA

"MY" Signature Louisiana 'Gospel Bird' (Fried Chicken) and Accompaniments Menu

-HIGHLIGHTS-

I. MENU

"MY" Signature Louisiana 'Gospel Bird' (Fried Chicken)
Hot Dipping Sauce
Smooth Leaf Mustard Greens and Neckbones
Cornbread
Pear Cobbler/ with Coconut Flakes
Louisiana Sweet Tea

II. RECIPES

"MY" Signature Louisiana 'Gospel Bird' (Fried Chicken) Recipe/ Hot Dipping Sauce

Amounts	Ingredients
2 cups	flour
2	eggs, large
2 tablespoons	olive oil
3 cups	vegetable oil

Directions

1. Wash chicken and pat dry.
2. Season Chicken
3. Divide flour into two bowls.

4. In a second bowl beat eggs with olive oil until frothy.
5. Dip each piece of chicken in the first bowl of flour.
6. Then dip in egg mixture. Shake off extra mixture.
7. Roll in the second bowl of flour.
8. Heat oil in deep fryer and Fry chicken until golden brown.

Hot Dipping Sauce

Amount	Ingredients
2cloves garlic,	minced
2	green onions, chopped
2 tablespoons	red wine vinegar
1 tablespoon	red chili pepper, ground
1 tablespoon	olive oil
½ teaspoon	salt
1 teaspoon	sugar
½ cup	water

Directions

1. Ground all ingredients up in food processor and serve.

ACCOMPANIMENTS

Louisiana Smooth Leaf Mustard Greens with Neckbones

Amount	Ingredients
1 pound	neckbones
2 quarts	water
3 bunches	smooth leaf mustards greens, washed and chopped
1 teaspoon	red pepper flakes
1 teaspoon	salt
1 tablespoon	sugar

Directions

1. In a large stockpot, boil neck bones in water until tender.
2. Gradually add in remaining ingredients.
3. Stir well and bring to a boil for 2 minutes. Then cook covered on medium heat for 2 hours.
4. Cool serve.

Louisiana Cornbread

Amount	Ingredients
2 cups	white cornmeal mix
1 cup	yellow meal
½ cup	sugar
2	eggs, slightly beaten
1 ½ cups	buttermilk
¼ cup	butter, melted

Directions

1. Preheat oven to 400 degrees F. Grease bread pan.
2. Mix dry ingredients together in a large bowl.
3. Mix in small bowl, eggs, buttermilk and butter.
4. Combine with dry ingredients and mix.
5. Pour into bread pan and bake for 15 minutes or until done.

Pear Cobbler with Coconut Flakes

Amount	Ingredients
1	prepared crust for 13 x 9x 2 – inch pan
2 pounds	pears, fresh, peeled and sliced
½ cup	brown sugar
1 cup	granulated sugar

1 teaspoon	salt
1 teaspoon	cinnamon
½ cup	water
1 cup	evaporated milk
1 cup	coconut flakes
¼ cup	butter, chopped

Directions

1. Preheat oven to 350 degrees F. Prepare cobbler crust for a 13 x 9 x 2 -inch pan and set aside.
2. In a large bowl, stir together all ingredients and pour in the bottom of the cobbler pan.
3. Place cobbler crust on top. Prick with a fork. Dot with butter on top.
4. Bake for 45 minutes or until golden brown.
5. Serve with ice cream.

Louisiana Sweet Tea

Amount	Ingredients
¼ cup	instant coffee
1 cup	instant tea
2 cups	sugar
2 quarts	hot water
1 quart	crushed ice

Directions

1. In a large bowl, dissolve coffee, tea and sugar in hot water. Stir well.
2. Add 1 quart of crushed ice. Serve.

III. GOSPEL MUSIC AND MUSICIANS

Mahalia Jackson

IV. WORSHIP MEETINGS PLACES ON THE PLANTATIONS

Church in Louisiana

"My old missus was good Catholic and she have us christened and make the first communion that not registered 'cause it before the freedom, but it were in old St. Martin's church what stand now. There was a statute of Pere Jean. The old priest in front of th church and one of St. Martin, too."
Ex-Slave Olivier Blanchard, Martinville, Louisiana

Church in Franklin Parish

"If a cullud man take de notion to preach 'bout de Gospel Dey didn't 'low him do dat. All he could 'bout wus obey de massa, obey dis, obey dat. Dey didn't make no passel of fuss 'bout prayin' den. Sometimes dey have prayin meetin' in a cabin at night. Each one bring de pot and put dere head in it to keep de echoes from gittin' back. Den dey pray in de pot. Dat de Gawd's truth."
E-Slave William Mathews, 89, Adam's Plantation

Church with the White Folks

"When Sunday came old massa ask who want to go to church. Dem what wants could ride hoss back or walk. Us go to de white folks church. Dey sat in front and us set in back. Us had prayer meetin', too, reg'lar every week. Old cullud man a sort of preacher. He de leader in 'legion.'"

Ex-Slave of Willian Lyons
Acadia Parish
Born in Branch, Louisiana

-OLDEST CHURCH IN LOUISIANA

First Colored Baptist Church in New Orleans. Established in 1872,

V. STATE FACTS

Louisiana

Origin of Name: In honour of Louis XIV of France

Entered union: April 30, 1812
Nickname: Pelican State
Capital -Baton Rouge
Motto: union, justice and confidence
State Symbols
Flower: magnolia
Tree: bald cypress
Bird: eastern brown pelican
Songs: :Give Me Louisiana"
You Are My Sunshine

VI. SCRIPTURES from the BIBLE

PSALM 23

The Lord is my shepherd; I shall not want
2. He maketh me to lie down in green pastures: he leadeth me by the still Waters.
3 He restoreth my soul: he leadeth me in the path of righteousness for his name's sake
4 Yea, though the I walk through the valley of the shadow of death, I will fear no evil for thou art with me: thy rod and thou staff they comfort me.

5 Thou prepared a table before me in the presence of mine enemies: thou anointed my head with oil;
My cup runneth over.

6 Surely goodness and mercy shall follow me all the days of my life: and I will dwell in the house of the LORD forever.

CHAPTER 7

MARYLAND

"MY" Signature Maryland 'Gospel Bird' (Fried Chicken) and Accompaniments Menu

-HIGHLIGHTS-

I. MENU

"MY" Signature Maryland 'Gospel Bird' (Fried Chicken)
Lemon Mustard Dipping Sauce
Collard Greens with Okra Pods
Cornbread
Cherry Cobbler
Maryland Sweet Tea

II. RECIPES

"MY" Signature Maryland 'Gospel Bird' (Fried Chicken) Recipe

Amount	Ingredients
2 pound	cut up fryer
1 quart	milk
1 teaspoon	salt
1 ½ teaspoons	black pepper
2 teaspoons	cumin
1 teaspoon	garlic granules
1 teaspoon	paprika
2 cups	flour
3 cups	oil for frying

Directions

1. Wash chicken and place in milk. Cover and refrigerate for 1 hour.
2. In a plastic bag, combine salt, black pepper, cumin, garlic granules, paprika and flour.
3. Shake well. Remove chicken from milk. Coat with flour mixture.
4. Fry in hot oil. Drain. Serve with dipping sauce.

Lemon-Mustard Dipping Sauce

Amounts	Ingredients
1 tablespoon	lemon juice
½ cup	mustard
¼ cup	brown sugar
1 cup	vinegar
1/ 4 cup	olive oil
1 teaspoon	garlic granules
¼ teaspoon	cayenne pepper
½ teaspoon	salt

Directions

1. Combine all ingredients in food processor.
2. Serve with hot fried chicken

ACCOMPANIMENTS

Collard Greens

Amount	Ingredients
1 pound	Maryland bacon, cubed
2 quarts	water
2 bunches	collard greens, washed, chopped

2	jalapeno peppers, chopped
2 teaspoons	salt
2 tablespoons	sugar
¼ cup	lard
10 pods	okra

Directions

1. In a large stockpot, boil meat and water until meat is tender.
2. Stir in collard greens and jalapeno pepper. Cook covered on medium heat for 45 minutes.
3. Stir in salt, sugar and lard.
4. Cover and cook for 30 minutes. Stir.
5. Lay pods of okra on top of collard greens and cook covered for 10 minutes on medium to low heat.

Skillet Cornbread

Amount	Ingredients
2 cups	yellow corn meal
½ cup	flour
2 teaspoons	baking powder
1 teaspoon	salt
1 cup	milk
1	egg, beaten
¼ cup	butter, melted

Directions

1. Place 2 tablespoons shortening in bottom of 12 -inch black iron skillet. Preheat oven to 400 degrees F. Heat skillet in oven for 2 minutes. Remove skillet from oven.
2. In a bowl, stir together corn meal, flour, baking powder and salt.

3. Make a well in the center. Set aside.
4. In a small bowl, mix together, milk, egg and butter. Stir into dry mixture.
5. Pour mixture in skillet and bake in oven for 25 minutes.

Cherry Cobbler

Amount	Ingredients
2 (300) cans	cherry pie filling
2 teaspoons	lemon juice
1 teaspoon	vanilla extract
½ cup	sugar
2 ½ cups	biscuit baking mix
1 teaspoon	cinnamon
1 cup	evaporated milk
1 cup	butter, chopped

Directions

1. Preheat oven to 350 degrees F.
2. In a large bowl, stir together cherry pie filling, lemon juice, vanilla extract and sugar.
3. Pour into bottom of a 13 x 9 x 2 -inch cobbler pan. Spread evenly. Set aside.
4. In a bowl, stir together biscuit baking mix and cinnamon. Toss in butter.
5. Sprinkle on top of cherry cobbler mixture.
6. Bake in oven for 30 minutes.

Maryland Sweet Tea

Amount	Ingredients
1 family size	tea bag
1 gallon	hot water

| 1 stick | cinnamon |
| 2 cups | sugar |

Directions

1. Steep tea bag in hot water. Remove tea bag.
2. Return to heat; add cinnamon stick and sugar and cook on low heat for 5-10 minutes.
3. Cool. Serve over ice.

III. GOSPEL MUSIC AND MUSICIANS

NOT KNOWN

IV. WORSHIP PLACES ON THE PLANTATIONS

"Mr. and Mrs. Dorsey conducted regular religion services of the Catholic Church on the farm in a chapel

Erected for that purpose and in which the slaves were taught the catechism and some learned how to

Read and write and were assisted by some catholic priests who came to the farm

On church and on Sundays for that purpose. When a child was born, it was baptized by the priests, and

Given names and ten were recorded in the Bible. We were taught the rituals of the Catholic church and when any one died. The funeral was conducted by a priest. The corpse was buried in the Dorsey graveyard a lot of about 1 ½ acres surrounded by cedar trees and well cared for. The only difference in the graves was that the Dorsey people had marble markers and the slaves had plain stones."

Ex-Slave Charles Coles
Baltimore, Maryland

OLDEST BLACK BAPTIST CHURCH IN MARYLAND

-The oldest black Baptist church in Maryland is First Baptist Church in Baltimore.

The church was established in 1836 by Rev. Moses C. Clayton

V. STATE FACTS

MARYLAND

Maryland-admitted to the April 28, 1788 (7th state)

Capital city: Annapolis
Nickname: Old Line State
Bird: Baltimore Oriole
Flower: Black-Eyed Susan
Tree: White Oak
State Drink: Milk
Dance: Square Dance
Maryland is named in honor of Henrietta Maria, wife of England's King Charles I
Song: "Maryland My Maryland".
Words By: James Ryder Randall
Music by: James Ryder Randall

VI. SCRIPTURES FROM THE BIBLE

MATTHEW 6:33

33 But seek ye first the Kingdom of God, and his righteousness and all these things shall be added unto you.

CHAPTER 8

MISSISSIPPI

"MY" Signature Mississippi 'Gospel Bird' (Fried
Chicken) And Accompaniments Menu

-HIGHLIGHTS-

I. MENU

"MY" Signature Mississippi 'Gospel Bird' (Fried Chicken)
Jerk
Dipping Sauce
Sliced Candied Yams
Mississippi Collard Greens
Mississippi Cornbread
"MY" Mississippi Berry Cobbler
Mississippi Sweet Tea

II. RECIPES

"MY" Signature Mississippi 'Gospel Bird' (Fried Chicken) Recipe/ Hot Barbeque Dipping Sauce

Amounts	Ingredients
2 pound	fryer, cut up
2 quarts	water
1 ½ teaspoons	seasoned salt
1 teaspoon	pepper
1 ½ teaspoons	garlic salt
2 ½ cups	self-rising flour

Directions

1. Cut up chicken, wash and boil for five minutes in sauce pan.
2. Cool down. Remove from water, Pat dry.
3. Combine seasoned salt, pepper, and garlic salt in a small bowl.
4. Season chicken.
5. Roll in flour,
6. Refrigerate for 2 hours.
7. When ready to cook, heat one-inch of cooking oil.
8. Fry until golden brown.

Hot Barbecue Dipping Sauce:

Amount	Ingredients
1 cup cider	vinegar
1 cup	tomato paste
1 ½ cups	tomato juice
¾ cup	dark brown sugar
1 ½ cups	molasses
1 cup	water
½ teaspoon	red pepper flakes
1 ½ teaspoons	whole cloves
1 stick	cinnamon
1 medium	onion, minced
1 clove	garlic, minced
2 teaspoons	salt
½ teaspoon	tabasco sauce
½ teaspoon	chili powder

Directions

1. Place all ingredients in a medium saucepan; stir well.
2. Cover and bring to a medium boil for 5 minutes.
3. Cool. Strain and serve warm.

ACCOMMPANIMENTS

Mississippi Collard Greens

Amounts	Ingredients
1 pound	cured turkey necks
2 quarts	water
2 bunches	collard greens, chopped
1	Harberno pepper, chopped
2 tablespoons	salt
¼ cup	lard

Directions

1. In a large stock pot, boil cured turkey necks in water until done. Remove from heat. Remove meat from necks and discard bones.
2. Return cured meat to pan, stir in remaining ingredients. Cover. Bring to a boil for 2-4 minutes and the return to medium heat. Stir. Cover and cook on low heat for 45 minutes.
3. Cook until desired doneness.

Candied Yams

Amount	Ingredients
2 pounds	Sweet potatoes, sliced
1 cup	butter
1 teaspoon	cinnamon
½ cup	sugar
½ cup	water
1 teaspoon	salt

Directions

1. Wash, peel and slice sweet potatoes horizontally. Set aside.

2. Melt butter in black skillet. Add sweet potatoes, cinnamon sugar and water.
3. Cover. Cook for 5 minutes and stir occasionally.
4. Add salt and stir. Cover and continue to cook until done.

Mississippi Cornbread

Amounts	Ingredients
2 cups	corn meal
½ cup	flour
3 teaspoons	baking powder
½ teaspoon	baking soda
1 teaspoon	salt
2 tablespoons	dark brown sugar
2	eggs, beaten
¼ cup	butter, melted
1 1/4 cups	buttermilk

Directions

1. Heat oven to 350 degrees F.
2. Grease 13 x 8 x2 -inch pan.
3. Combine corn meal, flour, baking powder, baking soda, salt and sugar Add eggs, butter and buttermilk.
4. Pour into prepared pan.
5. Bake for 35 minutes or until done.

MISSISSIPPI Blackberry Cobbler

Amounts	Ingredients
2 1/2 cups	blackberries
1 ½ cups	sugar
½ cup	flour

½ teaspoon	salt
2 tablespoons	corn starch
½ teaspoon	cinnamon
C1 teaspoon	lemon juice
½ cup	water

TOPPING

2 CUPS	All purpose flour
1 teaspoon	salt
1 ½ cups	ice cold butter, chopped
½ cup	milk
½ cup	pecans, chopped
½ cup	brown sugar
2 tablespoons	butter, melted

Directions

For Cobbler

1. Butter the sides and bottom of a 13 x 9 x inch pyrex pan.
2. Pick and wash blackberries. Set aside. Combine sugar, flour, salt, corn starch and cinnamon in a bowl and stir well. Toss in with blackberries. Add lemon juice and water. Gently stir and place in baking dish and spread evenly top with topping,

To Make Topping:

1. Combine flour and salt. Cut in butter until mixture makes coarse crumbs. Add milk and then roll out into 15 x 9-inch rectangular dough to fit top of pyrex dish. PRICK TOP WITH A FORK.
2. Place dough on top of blackberries in pyrex dish.
3. In a small bowl, combine pecans, brown sugar and butter.
4. Spread lightly on top of top.

5. 5, Bake for 35 minutes at 400 degrees F.

Mississippi Sweet Tea

Amount	Ingredients
2 family-size	tea bags
2 gallons	hot water
2 cans	frozen strawberry lemonade, thawed

Directions

1. In a large Stockpot, place tea bags and pour boiling water over tea bags.
2. Steep for 10 minutes and remove tea bags. Add sugar.
3. Stir until sugar is dissolved.
4. Gradually add thawed strawberry lemonade.
5. Serve over crushed ice.

-HIGHLIGHTS-

III.   GOSPEL MUSIC AND MUSICIANS

Popular musicians and ministers born in Mississippi.

Musicians Songs

1. Willie Banks, Raymond, Mississippi Look at the Blessings In the Name of Jesus
2. Bonner Brothers, Mississippi Delayed, But Not Denied
3. William Brothers Smithdale, Mississippi Never Let Go Of My Hand

Mama Prayed For Me

4. Mosie Burke Forest, Mississippi Oh, HAPPY DAY

5. Canton Spirituals -Canton, Mississippi
Keep Knocking
Too Late
Keep Blessing Me
6. Sam Cooke Clarksdale, Mississippi
Songs
1. Peace in the Valley
Just Another Day
Must Jesus Bear The Cross Along
Farther Along
7. Slim Hunter and the Supreme Angels Walnut Grove, Mississippi
Song- Glory to His Name
8. Ruby Terry Columbus, Miss
1.
Stand Still
Come to JESUS

MINISTERS/SINGERS

1. Reverend James Cleveland God' s ANSWERS
2. Reverend C.L. Franklin Sun Flower, Mississippi

Sermons

1. The 23rd Psalm
2. The Parodical Son
3. Two Fish and Five Loaves of Bread
4. King of the Jews
5. Ye are the Salt of the Earth
6. Lo I Am With You Always
7. All Good Things Work Together for the Good
8. Moses at the RED SEA

3. Rev. Gerald Thompson -Southaven, MISS -Let the Church
SAY AMEN

III.   WORSHIP MEETING PLACES ON THE PLANTATIONS

"Church on the Plantation"

"We had a neighborhood chu'ch an bofe black and white went to it. Dere was a white preacher an' sometimes a nigger preacher would set in the pulpit with him. De slsves saet on one side of the aisle an' white folks on de other. I allus liked preacher William Oden, an' his brudder DaNIEL, DE 'Slidin'Elder(1). Dey come from Ohio. Massa Bob Alen was head Steward. I 'member lots of my fav"'rite songs. Some of dem was, Am I Born to Die, Alas and Did My Savior Blestsed, bean' Must I to de Judgmen ge Brought. The Preacher would say "Pull down de line and let de spirit be a witness fer faith in de future frum high."

(1)   Back Slider
(2)   Ex-Slave Jim Allen, West Point, Mississippi

-OLDEST BLACK BAPTIST CHURCH IN MISSISSIPPI-

The Rose Hill Missionary Baptist Church in Natchez is the oldest black Baptist church in Mississippi. The church was created in 1854. C.L.

V.   STATE FACTS

Mississippi – A Southern State -20th State
Mississippi – Admitted to the Union December 10, 1817
Slave State 1817-1865 = 45 years

On the east-Alabama and Gulf of Mexico
On the south – LOUISIANA and Arkansas

State Abbreviation-MS
Capital: JACKSON
Name Origin: From an Indian word meaning "Father of Waters"
Motto: "Virtute et armis

(By valor and arms)
Nickname: Magnolia State
Hospitality State
Bird: Mockingbird
Butterfly: Spicebush Swallowtail
Fish: Largemouth Black BASS
Flower: Magnolia
Tree: Southern Magnolia
Song: "Go Mississippi"
Reptile: -American Alligator
Shellfish: Eastern Oyster
Large Mammal-White tailed deer

VI.   SCIPTURES FROM THE BIBLE

JOB 13:15

Though He slay me, yet will I trust in him, but I will maintain mine own ways

Before him.

CHAPTER 9

NORTH CAROLINA

"MY" Signature North Carolina 'Gospel Bird'
(Fried Chicken) and Accompaniments Menu

-HIGHLIGHTS-

I. MENU

"MY" Signature North Carolina 'Gospel Bird' (Fried Chicken)
Dipping Sauce
North Carolina Steamed Collard Greens
Corn Bread
Sweet Potato Cobbler
North Carolina Sweet Tea

II. RECIPES

"MY" Signature North Carolina -Gospel Bird' (Fried Chicken) Recipe

Amount	Ingredients
2 pound	fryer, cut up
2 ½ cups	flour
1 cup	cornmeal
1 teaspoon	cayenne pepper
2 teaspoons	salt
1 teaspoon	black pepper
1 teaspoons	garlic granules
1 teaspoon	chili powder
3 cups	oil for frying

Directions

1. Wash and cut up chicken. Set aside
2. In a large bowl, combine flour, corn meal and seasonings. Stir well.
3. Coat chicken and fry in oil until golden brown.

Hickory Dipping Sauce

Amount	Ingredients
1 cup	apple cider vinegar
½ teaspoon	liquid smoke
2 cups	barbecue sauce
1 teaspoon	chili powder
3 tablespoons	honey
2 tablespoons	mustard
1 cup	water

Directions

1. Add all ingredients together in a medium saucepan. Stir well.
2. Heat over medium heat for ten minutes. Cool. Serve.

ACCOMPANIMENTS

North Carolina Steamed Collard Greens

Amount	Ingredients
2 quarts	water
2 bunches	collard greens, chopped
1	yellow onions, chopped
2 pounds	cured North Carolina link sausages, sliced
1 teaspoon	salt

| ½ teaspoon | red pepper flakes |
| ¼ cup | lard |

Directions

1. In a large stockpot, boil water and add collard greens. Cover and cook for 30 minutes.
2. Stir in remaining ingredients.
3. Taste for doneness.

Spicy Cornbread

Amount	Ingredients
2 ½ cups	cornmeal
¼ cup	flour
2 teaspoons	baking powder
1 tablespoon	sugar
1 teaspoon	salt
1 ½ cups	buttermilk
1	eggs, beaten
¼ cup	melted butter
1	jalapeno pepper, chopped

Directions

1. Preheat oven to 400 degrees F. Grease bread pan.
2. In a large bowl, sift together dry ingredients
3. In a second bowl, beat together liquid ingredients.
4. Carefully stir into dry ingredients. Stir in jalapeno pepper.
5. Pour into bread pan. Bake for 30 minutes or until done.

Sweet Potato Cobbler

Amount	Ingredient
2 prepared	cobbler crusts for 13 x 9 x 2-inch pan
1 pound	sweet potatoes, peeled, cubed
¾ cup	brown sugar
¼ cup	sugar
½ teaspoon	nutmeg
1 teaspoon	cinnamon
1 cup	evaporated milk
1 teaspoon	lemon juice
½ cup	butter, melted

Directions

1. Preheat oven to 350 degrees F. Place bottom crust in the cobbler pan. Prick bottom crust. Set aside.
2. 2, In a large bowl, mix together sweet potatoes, sugars, nutmeg, cinnamon, evaporated milk and lemon juice Pour into cobbler pan on top of crust.
3. Spread mixture out evenly. Pour melted butter over mixture.
4. Place top crust over mixture. Prick holes in top crust. Bake for 20 minutes.

North Carolina Sweet Tea

Amount	Ingredients
2 family size	red pekoe tea
1 gallon	water
2 cups	sugar
3	lemons, sliced

Directions

1. Steep red tea in hot water for 10 minutes. Remove tea bags. Dissolve sugar.
2. Add lemons and serve over ice.

- HIGHLIGHTS-

III. GOSPEL MUSIC AND MUSICIANS

1. Inez Andrews – Rocky Mount, North Carolina
2. Shirley Ceasar-
3. The McDonald Sister-Fayetteville, North Carolina
4. Rev. F.C. Barnes Rocky Mount

Songs

-Come on in the room
The Old Time Way
He Want Change
Get's Right Church

5. Luther Barnes Rocky Mount
Some One to Lean

IV. WORSHIP PLACES ON THE PLANTATION

"We were allowed to have prayer meetings in our homes and we also went to the white folks church.

"They would not teach any of us to read and write. Books and papers

Ex-Slave Mary Anderson
Born on a plantation
Wake County, N.C.
May 10, 1851

-OLDEST BLACK CHURCH IN NORTH CAROLINA SHAW UNIVRSITY located in Raleigh, North Carolina

Founded in 1865 by an ex-slave.

V. STATE FACTS

NORTH CAROLINA
North Carolina-
Nickname: Tar Heel State
Entered Union: Nov 12, 1789
Tree: Pine
Motto: Esse quana videro (to be
State Symbols
Flower: dogwood
Bird: Cardinal
Mammal: gray squirrel
Insect: honey bee
Largest City: Charlotte
Border states:

South Carolina and Georgia to the South;
Tennessee to the West;
Virginia to the North and the Atlantic Ocean to the east.

Song: "The Old North State"
Colors: red and blue
Fruit: scuppernong grape

VI. SCRIPTURES from the BIBLE

MATTHEW 6:6-15

6 But thou, when thou prayest, enter into thy closet, and when thou hast shut thy door, pray to thy Father which is in secret; and thy Father, which seeth in secret shall reward thee openly.

7 But hen ye pray, use not vain repetitions, as the heathen do, for they think that they shall be heard for their much speaking.

8 Be not ye therefore like unto them: for your Father knoweth what things ye have need of, before ye ask him.

9 After this manner therefore pray ye Our Father which art in heaven Hallowed be thy name.

10 Thy kingdom come. Thy will be done in earth, as it is in heaven.

11. Give us this day our daily bread.

12 And forgive us our debts, as we forgive our debtors.

13 And lead us not into temptation, but deliver us from evil, for thy is the kingdom, and the power, and the glory, for ever. Amen.

14. For if ye forgive men their trespasses, neither will your Father forgive your trespasses.

15But if ye forgive not men their trespasses, neither will your Father forgive your trespasses.

CHAPTER 10

OKLAHOMA

"MY" Signature Oklahoma 'Gospel Bird' (fried
Chicken) and Accompaniment Menu

-HIGHLIGHTS-

I. MENU

"MY" Signature Oklahoma 'Gospel Bird' (Fried Chicken)
Cowboy Dipping Sauce
Stewed Turnip Greens/Bottoms/ Dumplings
Hoecake Patties
Dewberry Cobbler
Oklahoma Brewed Lemon-Sweet Tea

II. RECIPES

"MY" Signature Oklahoma 'Gospel Bird' (Fried Chicken) Recipe

AMOUNTS	INGREDIENTS
2 1/2 pounds	fryer, cut up
1 ½ teaspoons	salt
2 teaspoons	garlic powder
1 ½ teaspoons	onion powder
1 teaspoon	black pepper
3 cups	all-purpose flour
2 cups	shortening, for frying

Directions

1. Clean and wash cut-up chicken. Set aside.

2. Place seasonings in small bowl and stir well.
3. Place flour in plastic bag.
4. Season each piece of chicken separately.
5. Roll in flour.
6. Heat shortening up in cast iron skillet to 325 degrees F.
7. Fry until golden brown on each side

Cowboy Dipping Sauce

Amount	Ingredients
½ cup	hot sauce
1 small	onion, chopped
1 tablespoon	Worcestershire Sauce
1 cup	cocktail sauce
1 tablespoon	mustard
1 cup	apple cider vinegar
¼ cup	brown sugar
½ cup	catsup

Directions

1. In a large saucepan, heat all ingredients for 10 minutes.
2. Cool and chop in food processor.

ACCOMPANIMENTS

Stewed Turnip Greens/Bottoms/ Cornmeal Dumplings

Amount	Ingredients
1 quart	water
½ pound	salt pork, cubed
1 bunch	turnip greens, washed and chopped
1 pound	turnip bottoms or roots, chopped

1 medium	yellow onion, diced
1 teaspoon	salt
½ teaspoon	red pepper flakes

Dumplings:

2 cups	cornmeal, white
1 tablespoon	flour
½ teaspoon	salt
¾ cup	water

Directions

1. In a large stockpot, place water and salt pork. Cover. Cook salt pork in water over medium heat until tender.
2. Remove top from saucepot and stir in greens and cook for 30 minutes.
3. Stir in turnip bottoms, yellow onion, salt and red pepper. Cover and
4. Cook for an additional 15 minutes.
5. Make dumplings: Stir together cornmeal, flour and salt.
6. Stir in water. Hand make 12 small balls.
7. Carefully place each ball on top of boiling turnip greens and bottom mixture. Cover and cook for 10 minutes. Donot stir.
8. Serve.

Hoecake Patties Cornbread

Amount	Ingredients
3 cups	cornmeal
½ cup	flour
1 teaspoon	baking powder
1 teaspoon	salt
1	egg slightly beaten

½ cup	milk
½ cup	water
	Vegetable oil for frying

Directions

1. In a medium bowl, combine cornmeal, flour, baking powder and salt. Set aside.
2. In a second bowl, combine egg, milk and water.
3. Combine liquid ingredients in the center of the cornmeal mixture.
4. Heat oil in cast iron skillet to 350 degrees F.
5. Place ¼ cup mixture of cornmeal mixture and fry each hoecake.

Dewberry Cobbler

Amount	Ingredients
2	pie crust for 13 x 9 x 2 -inch pan (cobbler pan)
3 cups	dewberries
1 cup	sugar
½ teaspoon	cinnamon
¼ cup	flour
½ cup	water
1 teaspoon	salt
2 teaspoons	lemon juice
½ cup	butter, chopped

Directions

1. Preheat oven to 400 degrees F. Place one crust in bottom of the cobbler pan. Prick with fork. Bake in oven till golden brown. Remove from oven. Cool.

2. In a large bowl, toss together dewberries, sugar, cinnamon, flour, water, cinnamon, salt, and lemon juice. Spread dewberry mixture over cooled cobbler crust.
3. Dot butter over mixture. Place second crust on top of mixture.
4. Prick holes in crust.
5. Bake at 350 degrees F. or until done.

Oklahoma Brewed Lemon -Sweet Tea

Amount	Ingredients
2 family size	orange pekoe tea bags
2 gallons	water
4	whole cloves
3 cups	sugar
½ cup	lemon juice, freshly squeezed

Directions

1. Boil tea bags in water for 10 minutes. Remove bags and add whole cloves. Simmer for 5 minutes. Remove whole cloves. Stir in sugar. Cool. Add lemon juice.
2. Stir well. Serve over ice.

III.   GOSPEL MUSIC AND MUSICIANS

NOT KNOWN

IV. WORSHIP ON THE PLANTATION

Church on the Plantation

"The master had a brother who used to preach to the negroes on the sly. One time he was caught and the master hipped him something awful."

Ex-Slave Nancy Rogers Bens
Hulbert, Oklahoma.

V. STATE FACTS

OKLAHOMA

Nickname: Sooner State

Origin of the Name of Oklahoma: The name Oklahoma is from the Choctaw, Indian words "Okla" meaning people and "homa" meaning red.

Statehood: November 16, 1907; 46th state

State Capital: Oklahoma City

Largest City: Oklahoma City

Number of Counties:77

Bordering States: Arkansas, Colorado, Kansas, Missouri, New Mexico, Texas

State Motto: "Labor omner Vinist:" Labor Conquers All Things

State Song: "Oklahoma" Rodgers Hammerstein

State Bird: Scissor-Tailed Flycatcher

State Animal: Buffalo

State Game Mammal: White-tailed deer

State Fish: White or Sand Bass

State Butterfly: Black Swallow Tail

State Floral Emblem- Mistletoe

State Flower – Oklahoma Rose

State Wildflower – Indian Blanket

State Tree- Red bud

State Grass – Indian grass

State Beverage -Milk

State Colors: Green and white

Major Rivers: Arkansas River, Canadian River, Red River

VI.   SCRIPTURES from the BIBLE

6 In all thy ways acknowledge him, and he shall direct thy paths.

7 Be not wise in thine own eyes: Hear the Lord with plenty and thy presses shall burst out with new wine.

1. Be not wise in thine own eyes fear the Lord, and depart from evil.
2. Honour the Lord with thy substance, and with the first fruits of thine increase.
3. So shall thy barns be filled with plenty and thy presses shall burst out with new wine.

CHAPTER 11

SOUTH CAROLINA

"MY" Signature South Carolina 'Gospel Bird' (Fried Chicken) and Accompaniments Menu

-HIGHLIGHTS-

I. MENU

"MY" Signature South Carolina 'Gospel Bird' (Fried Chicken)
Low -Country Dipping Sauce
Savory Collard Greens
Carolina Hoppin Johns
Surprise Cornbread
Red Peaches Cobbler
South Carolina Sweet Tea

II. RECIPES

'MY" Signature South Carolina 'Gospel Bir' (Fried Chicken) Recipe

Amount	Ingredients
1-21/2 pounds	chicken, cut up
1 quart	milk
2 cups	buttermilk
2	eggs, slightly
1 teaspoon	hot sauce
½ teaspoon	black pepper
5 cups	self-rising flour
3 cups	shortening

Directions

1. Wash chicken and soak in milk for one hour.
2. In a separate bowl, combine buttermilk, eggs and hot sauce.
3. In a bowl, stir together black pepper and self-rising flour.
4. Drain milk from cut-up chicken.
5. Dip chicken pieces in flour mixture and
6. Then roll in flour. Shake excess flour.
7. Heat up shortening and fry to golden brown on both sides.
8. Drain.

Low Country Dipping Sauce

Amounts	Ingredients
½ cup	apple cider vinegar
2 tablespoons Dijohn mustard	
3 tablespoons	Worcestershire sauce
1 tablespoons	lime juice
1 teaspoon	salt
1 teaspoon	pepper
1 teaspoon	old bay seasoning
1 teaspoon	garlic minced
2 tablespoons	Italian Dressing
1 cup	honey barbecue sauce

Directions

1. Properly measure all ingredients and blenderize. Serve as dipping sauce.

ACCOMPANIMENTS

Savory Collard Greens

Amounts	Ingredients
1 quart	water
6 cured	turkey necks
2 bunches	collards, cut up
2 tablespoons	canola oil
½ teaspoon	red pepper flakes
1 tablespoon	salt
2 tablespoons	sugar

Directions

1. In a large, boiling pot boil water and turkey necks until tender. and cool.
2. Keep broth and add 2 cups water. Stir well.
3. Remove meat from necks and chop. Add meat to water.
4. Stir in greens and remaining ingredients
5. Boil for 21/2 hours until tender.
6. Serve with cornbread.

Carolina Hoppin' Johns

Amounts	Ingredients
1 pound bag	black eyed peas
1	ham hock, cut up
½ cup	onions, chopped
1/2 teaspoon	red pepper flakes
2 teaspoons	salt
2 quarts	water
4 cups	white rice, cooked

Directions

1. Pick and wash dried black- eyed peas.
2. In a large stock pot, place black-eyed peas, ham hock, onions red pepper flakes and salt
   In water cover and bring to a boil. Boil on medium and stir constantly until desired doneness.
3. Stir in cooked rice and continue to cook on low until heated thoroughly. Serve.

Surprise Cornbread

Amounts	Ingredients
1 pkg	yeast
1/3 cup	warm water
3 cups	all-purpose flour
2 cups	white corn meal
1 teaspoon	baking soda
4 teaspoons	baking powder
¼ cup	salt
1 cup	shortening
¼ cup	butter
2 cups	buttermilk

Directions

1. Preheat oven to 400 degrees F.
2. In a bowl, dissolve yeast in warm water and set aside.
3. Mix together flour, meal, baking soda, baking powder, sugar, and salt.
4. Mix in butter and shortening well into flour mixture.
5. Add yeast mixture and buttermilk.
6. Roll out onto floured surface into ½-inch thickness.

7. Cut out and place on a greased cookie sheet.
8. Bake 15-18 minutes until done.
9. Serve hot.

Red Peaches Cobbler

Amounts	Ingredients
4 pounds	red peaches, sliced
1 cup	granulated white sugar
1 cup	brown sugar
½ teaspoon	cinnamon
1 teaspoon	salt
3 tablespoons	flour
¼ teaspoon	allspice
¼ cup	milk
1/ cup	butter, thinly sliced
2 prepared	crusts for 9 x 13 x 2 pan

Directions

1. Preheat oven to 350 degrees F.
2. Grease a 13 x 9 x 2 inch pan. Line pan with one pie crust. Prick holes in pie crust. Set aside.
3. Prepare peaches. Set aside.
4. Mix together remaining ingredients in a large bowl.
5. Stir in peaches.
6. Pour peach mixture into lined pan with pie crust.
7. Top peaches with second crust. Prick holes in top of crust.
8. Bake in oven for 40 minutes or until desired doneness.

Carolina Sweet Tea

Amount	Ingredients
1 gallon	water
2 family	tea bags
2 cups	sugar
1 teaspoon	vanilla extract

Directions

1. In a large stockpot, boil water for 2 minutes. Remove from heat.
2. Add tea bags. Let stand for 5 minutes. Remove tea bags and stir in sugar and vanilla extract.
3. Serve over ice.

-HIGHLIGHTS-

III. GOSPEL MUSIC AND MUSICIANS

Musicians	Place of Birth
Margaret Allison	Phim Branch

Song
Touch Me Lord Jesus

Rev. Julius Cheeks	Spartanburg, South Carolina

Song
Somebody Left on the Morning Train

Dixie Hummingbirds	Greenville, SC

Songs

1. I Know My Redeemer Lives
2. Heaven's Grocery Store

Doc Mackensie and the Gospel HiLites

Olanto, South Carolina
Song
He is Coming Back

IV. WORSHIP ON THE PLANTATION

MOTHER BORNED AGAIN

"When I got to be a big boy, my ma got religion as us camp meeting at El- Bethel. She shouted and sung for three days, going all over de plantation and de neighboring one, inviting her friends to come to see her baptizing and shouting and praying for dem. She went around to all de people dat she had done wronged her and told dem dat she was born again and a new woman, and dat she would forgive dem. She wanted everybody dat was not saved to go up wid her.

"De white folks was baptized in de pool first, and den dere darkies. When de darkies times come, dey sung and shouted so loud dat patter-rollers come from somewhar, but marster and missus made dem go away and let us shout and rejoice to de fullest.

:Missus had all her darkies to wear white calico in de pool dat was a -gwine in fer baptizing.

"In de serving -room she had calico robes made fer everybody. My ma took me wid her to see her baptized, and I eas so happy dat I sung and shouted wid her. All de nigger -jined in singing. De white folks stamyed and saw us baptized our folks and dey liked our singing"

Source: Isaiah Jefferies
Gaffney, S.C. (age 86)

ANOTHER SLAVE'S ACCOUNT

"I went to White Pop;ar Springs Church, de Baptist church my mistrss tended. De preacher was Mr. Cartledge. He allowed Miss Marion was de flower of his flock.

"Slaves lived in quarters, a stretch of small houses off de white houses. Patrollers often come to search for stray slaves wouldn't take your word for it. They would for it. They would search de house. If they ketch one widout a pass, they whipped him. We got most our outside newa SunSay at CHURCH, WHEN farm work was not pressing, on Saturday, we got all clean 'round de house and

Wash and iron our clothes.

Ex-Slave Adelina Jackson, 86
Winnsboro, S.C.

-OLDEST BLACK BAPTIST CHURCH IN SOUTH CAROLINA-

The Silver Bluff Baptist Church in South Carolina.
The first black Baptist congregation in South Carolina in 177# on the Galpin Plantation in Silver Bluff was founded by Rev. West Palmer a white Connecticut minister and an African-American pastor George Liele.

The plantation was located 14 miles northwest of Savannah, Georgia.

V. STATE FACTS

SOUTH CAROLINA

Nickname: Palmetto State
South CaROLINA WAS NAMED AFTER King Charles I
Joined the Union : May 3, 1788
8th State
Slave State for: 77 years
Capital: Columbia
Motto: Dum Spio Spero (While I breathe, I Hope)

Animal: Whitetail deer
Beverage: Milk
Bird: Carolina Wren
Butter fly: Eastern tiger Swallow tail butterfly
Dance: The Shag

Dog: Boykin Spaniel
Fish: Striped Bass
Flower:: Yellow Jessamine
Folk Dance: The Square Dance
Fruit: Peach
Number of Counties: 46

Game Bird: Wild Turkey
Gemstone: Amethyst
Hospitality Beverage: Tea
Insect: Carolina Mantis
Reptile: Loggerhead Turtle

Tree: Sabal Palmetto
Fort Sumter: Place Where first shot was fired to start the Civil
War=1861-1865.

South Carolina is known for Gullah, a culture from Africa. The Gullah tradition is practiced in the Sea Islands of South Carolina and Georgia. South Carolina Sea Islands- Daufaskie. Sullivan, Edisto, James, Morris, Folly, Seabrppk, St. Helena Island, Friipp IslAND, Port Royal Island

VI. SCRIPTURES from the Bible

LUKE 4:15-18

15 And he taught in their synagogues, being glorified of all.

16 And he came to Nazareth, where he had been brought up: and as his custom was, he went into the synagogue on the sabbath day, and stood up for to read.

And there was delivered unto him the book of the prophet Esais. And when he had opened the book, he found the place where it was written.

18 The Spirit of the Lord is upon me, because he hath anointed me to preach the gospel to the poor; he hath sent me to hel the broken-hearted, to preach deliverance to the captives, and recovering of sight to the blind, to set at liberty them that are bruised.

19 To preach the acceptable year of the Lord.

CHAPTER 12

TENNESSEE

"MY" Signature Tennessee 'Gospel Bird' (Fried Chicken) and Accompaniment Menu

-HIGHLIGHTS-

I. MENU

"MY" Signature Tennessee 'Gospel Bird' (Fried Chicken)
Orange Dipping Sauce
Old -Fashioned Collard Greens
Tennessee Cracklin Bread
Plum and Apple Cobbler
Tennessee Sweet Tea

II. RECIPES

"MY" Signature Tennessee 'Gospel Bird' (Fried Chicken) Recipe

Amount	Ingredients
2 ½ pounds	fryer, cut up
2 cups	apple cider vinegar
2 tablespoons	salt until salt is dissolved. Cool down.
2 quarts	water
2	eggs, beaten
Cups	buttermilk
2 ½ cups	flour
1 teaspoon	paprika
1 teaspoon	garlic salt
1 ½ teaspoons	black pepper
3 cups	shortening
½ cup	lard

Directions

1. Pick and wash chicken. Set aside
2. Combine vinegar, salt and water. Heat on range.
3. Cool down. Pour over chicken. Cover and refrigerate for 30 minutes.
4. Pour off brine. Wash chicken in cool water. Pat dry.
5. Combine butter milk and egg in a bowl stir well. Combine flour, paprika, garlic and black pepper in a plastic bag.
6. Roll each piece of chicken in buttermilk mixture. Then roll in seasoned flour.
7. Shake off excess seasoned flour seasoned flour.
8. Fry in hot shortening and lard.

Orange Dipping Sauce

Amount	Ingredients
½ cup	orange juice
1 cup	cane syrup
2 tablespoons	Teriyaki sauce
½ cup	barbecue sauce
2 tablespoons	ketchup

Directions

1. Measure all ingredients in medium sauce pan. Stir well. Bring to a boil; cover, and simmer for 5 minutes.
2. Cool and serve.

ACCOMPANIMENTS

Old -Fashioned Collard Greens

Amount	Ingredients
2	pig-tails, country cured
1 quart	water

2 bunches	collard greens, picked, washed and ut-up
2 tablespoons	oil
1 teaspoon	red pepper flakes
1 teaspoon	salt

Directions

1. Wash pig's tails and cut into 2 inch pieces. Cook pig tails in the water in a large pot.
2. Boil until tender. Stir in collard greens.
3. Bring to a boil for 2-3 minutes; cover and simmer for 30 minutes.
4. Add remaining ingredients and cook for 1 hour or until desired doneness.

Tennessee Cracklin' Bread

Amount	Ingredients
1 cup	corn meal
½ cup	all-purpose flour
1 tablespoon	sugar
1 tablespoon	baking soda
1 teaspoon	salt
1 ½ cups	buttermilk
1	egg, slightly beaten
½ cup	cracklins, fried meat skins, chopped

Directions

1. Preheat oven to 400 degrees F. Grease baking pan.
2. Sift together cornmeal, all-purpose flour, sugar, baking soda and salt.
3. In a bowl, combine buttermilk and egg.

4. Stir together cornmeal mixture and buttermilk mixture. Stir in cracklins'

5. Pour into baking pan.

6. Bake for 20 minutes.

Apple and Plum Cobbler

Amount	Ingredients
2 pounds	cooking apples, peeled, cored and sliced
½ teaspoon	cinnamon
2 tablespoons	flour
1 pound	green plums, peeled, cored and sliced.
1 cup	raisins
2 cups	sugar
2 teaspoons	lemon juice
1 teaspoon	vanilla extract
½ cup	butter, sliced
3	prepared pie crusts for 13 x 9 x 2 inch pan

Directions

1. Preheat oven to 350 degrees F. Grease 13 x 9 x 2 inch baking dish. Place one crust in bottom of pan. Prick bottom.

2. In a one bowl, combine apples, cinnamon, flour, 1 cup sugar and 1 teaspoon lemon juice.

3. Pour mixture over crust in pan. Roll 2nd crust on top of apple mixture. Set aside.

4. In a 2nd bowl, combine green plums and raisins. Add 1 teaspoon lemon juice. Vanilla extract and butter. Stir well and then add one cup of sugar.

5. Place third crust on top and make pricks in crust. Bake for 50 minutes or until golden brown.

Tennessee Sweet Tea

Amount	Ingredients
2 packages family size	tea
2 quarts	water
1 cup	sugar
1 quart	pineapple/ orange juice mixture

Directions

1. Boil water and ad tea bags for 5 minutes. Remove tea bags and add sugar. Stir until melted. Cool done and then ad orange/ pineapple juice. Stir well.
2. Chill 30 minutes before serving.

-HIGHLIGHTS-

III. GOSPEL MUSIC AND MUSICIANS

Musicians Hometown

1. Rev. Clay Evans Brownsville, Tennessee

Songs

1. At the Cross
2. I'm Blessed
3. I'm Going Through
4. Something About God's Grace
5. Lord Make Me Right
6. Room At The Cross

2. Aretha Franklin Memphis, Tennessee

IV.   WORSHIP on the PLANTATION

1.   Baptist Church

"I 'longs ter de goter camp-meetin's an hab a big time wid good thingster eat. Didn't goter de baptizin' much. Dey would leave de chuch singin' en shoutin'. Dere ez three days in September dat we hab dinnah on de groun' en all Baptist git tergedder. We calls hit de 'sociation."

Ex-Slave Julian Casey
Nashville, Tennessee

-OLDEST BLACK BAPTIST CHURCH IN TENNESSEE-

Spruce Street Baptist Church-1835
Nashville, Tennessee

V.   STATE FACTS

TENNESSEE

Joined the Union: June 1, 1796
Slave State: 59 years
State Capital: Nashville
State Nickname: "The Volunteer State"
State Motto "Agriculture and Commerce"
Number of Counties: 95
Bordering States: Alabama, Arkansas, Georgia, Kentucky, Mississippi, Missouri, North Carolina and Virginia
Origin of the Name: The name Tennessee came from a Cherokee Village in the region that is called "Tanasie".
Geographical Regions: 1-The Great Smoky Mountains

2.   The Highlands
3.   Low Lands

State Songs: My Homeland Tennessee
The Tennessee Waltz
When It's Iris Time in Tennessee
My Tennessee
Rocky Top
Tennessee
The Pride of Tennessee
State Bird: Mockingbird
State Game Bird: Bobwhite quail
State Wild Animal: Racoon
State Insects: Firefly and Ladybug
State Butterfly: Zebra Swallowtail
State Amphibian: Tennessee Cave Salamander
State Sport Fish: Largemouth Bass
State commercial Fish: Channel Catfish
State Flower: Iris
State Wildflower: Passion flower
State Tree: Tulip poplar
State Gem: Tennessee River Pearl
State Rocks: Limestone and Agate
State Folk Dance: Square Dance

VI.   SCRIPTURES from the BIBLE

PSALM 119:133-135
133 Order my steps in thy word and let not any iniquity have dominion over me.

134 Deliver me from the oppression of man; so will I keep so will I keep thy precepts.

135 Make thy face to shine upon thy servant; and teach me thy statutes.

CHAPTER 13

TEXAS

"MY" Signature Texas 'Gospel Bird' (Fried
Chicken) And Accompaniments Menu

-HIGHLIGHTS-

I. MENU

"MY" Signature Texas 'Gospel Bird' (Fried Chicken)
Jalapeno Dipping Sauce
Texas Chicken and Dressing
Texas Collard Greens
Texas Cornbread
Texas Cobbler
Texas Sweet Tea

II. RECIPES

"MY' Signature Texas 'Gospel Bird" Fried Chicken Recipe

Amounts	Ingredients
1	3-31/2 pound fryer, cut-up Marinade
4 cups	buttermilk
¼ cup	vinegar, distilled Seasoning
1 teaspoon	salt
1 teaspoon	black pepper
½ teaspoon	paprika
1 teaspoon	cumin
½ teaspoon	chili powder
2 cups	self-rising flour
4 cups	vegetable oil

Directions

1. Wash and pat dry cut-up chicken.
2. Place in plastic bowl buttermilk and vinegar. Stir well. Coat chicken with mixture cover and refrigerate 2 to 3 hours.
3. Combine seasoning and flour in a large bowl.
4. Remove chicken from bowl and roll in flour mixture.
5. Heat oil in a deep fryer.
6. Fry chicken to golden brown.
7. Drain. Serve with dipping sauce

Jalapeno Dipping Sauce

Amount	Ingredients
2	jalapeno peppers, seeds removed
2cups	Ranch dressing
2 tablespoons	hot sauce
3 tablespoons	cane syrup

Directions

1. Place all ingredients in food processor, and blend.
2. Serve.

ACCOMPANIMENTS

Texas Chicken and Dressing

Amount	Ingredients
4 cups	cornmeal mix
1 teaspoon	sage
1 teaspoon	black pepper
3 cups	chicken broth
1 -300 can	celery soup

1-300 can	mushroom soup
3	eggs, slightly beaten
1 cup	onion, minced
¼ cup	green pepper, minced
1 cup	celery, minced
3 cups	wheat bread, cubed

Directions

1. Make corn meal mix according to package directions. Crumble bread.
2. In a large bowl, beat together all ingredients.
3. Place in a large greased baking dish and bake at 374 degrees F. for 30-40 minutes.

ACCOMPANIMENTS

Texas Collard Greens

Amounts	Ingredients
4	turkey wings cured chopped
1 quart	water
2 bunches	collard greens, washed and chopped
1	jalapeno pepper, chopped
1 quart	water
4	bouillon cubes, chicken
2 tablespoons	shortening
1 teaspoon	red pepper flakes
1-2 teaspoons	salt

Directions

1. In large stockpot, boil turkey wings until tender. Set aside.

2. Prepare collard greens and pepper. Set aside. Dissolve the chicken bouillon cubes by boiling the second quart of the water.
3. Using the large stockpot, combine all ingredients together, except salt. Stir well. Cook covered for 45 minutes on low heat and then add salt.
4. Stir well and return to heat and cook for an additional 5 minutes.

Texas Corn Bread

Amounts	Ingredients
1 cup	self-rising flour
11/2 cups	corn meal
3 tablespoon	sugar
2	eggs, slightly beaten
1 cup	buttermilk
¼ cup	shortening, melted
½ cup	onions, chopped
¼ cup	bell pepper
½ cup	creamed corn

Directions

1. Preheat oven to 400 degrees. F. Grease bread pan.
2. In a large bowl. sift together all dry ingredients. Set aside. In a second bowl, mix together remaining ingredients and then stir in the center of the meal mixture.
3. Pour into prepared pan. Bake for 15-29 minutes.

Texas Cobbler

Amount	Ingredients
2-	phyllo crust, one for bottom and top
1- 300 can	cherry pie filling

1-can	300 can apple pie filling
1/2 teaspoon	cinnamon
½ cup	butter, sliced
2 tablespoons lemon juice	

Directions

1. Preheat oven to 350 degrees F.
2. Place one of the phyllo crust in the bottom of a greased 13 x 9 x 2 pan. Set aside.
3. In a large bowl mix together remaining ingredients. Place in phyllo crust. Layer top with second crust.
4. Bake for 30 minutes at 350 degrees F.

Texas Sweet Tea

Amount	Ingredients
1 gallon	boiling water
1 stick	cinnamon
1 Whole	allspice
5	lemon slices
2 family size	tea bags
3 cups	sugar

Directions

1. In a large stockpot boil water, cinnamon and allspice for 5 minutes. Cool add lemon slices, tea bags. Steep for 15 minutes. Remove all materials from stock pot. Stir in sugar.
2. Serve over ice.

HIGHLIGHTS

III. GOSPEL MUSIC AND MUSCIANS

Musician Hometown
Kirk Franklin Fort Worth, Texas

Songs

1. Melodies from Heaven
2. Don't Take Your Joy Away
3. Silver and Gold
4. Till We Meet Again

IV. WORSHIP on the PLANTATION

Church in Texas

"My missus took us chillen to de Baptis' Church and de white preacher he preach. De cullud folks could have church demselves effen dey have de manager of 'ligion to kindr preach. Course he couldn't read just talk what he done heard de white preachers say."

Ex-Slave Louis Love, 91
Orange, Texas

"I been preachin' the Gospel and farmin' since slavery time. I jned the church mos' 83 years ago when I was Major Gand;s slave and they baptizes me in the spring branch ccloset to ehrtr I finds the Lord's.

When I started to preach I couldn't read or write and had to preach what massa told me and he say tell them niggers iffen they obey the massa dey goes to Heaven but I knowed there's something better for them, but daren't tell them 'cept on the sly. That I done lots I tells 'em iffen they keppa prayin' the Lord will set 'em free. But since them days I's done studied some and I preached and over Panola and Harrison County and I started Edward's Chapel over there in Marshall and pastored it till a few years ago. It's named for me."

Ex-Slaves Anderson and Minerva Edwards
Marshall, Texas

– OLDEST BLACK BAPTIST HURCH IN TEXAS

First Baptist Church establish in 18 67 in Houston and Galveston area.

V.   STATE FACTS

TEXAS

Admission to the Union:
December 29, 1845 *28th state)

Slave State from 1845-1865*Juneteeth)
20 years
(Second largest state in the United States and located in South Central region in United States.)
Texas –
Nickname: The Lone Star State
Motto: Friendship
State Song: "Texas, Our Texas"
Capital: Austin
Largest City: Houston
Border States:
To the East: Louisiana
Northeast: Arkansas
North: Oklahoma
West: New Mexico

Bordered by the Mexico states of Chihuahua, Coahuela, Nuevo Leon, Tammmaulipas to the southwest.

The Gulf of Mexico is to the southeast.

State Flower: Bluebonnet
State Tree: Pecan
State Bird: Northern Mockingbird
State Mammal: Nine banded Armadillo
State Mammal (large) Texas Longhorn

State Mammal (flying) Mexican tailed bat
State Insect: Monarch Butterfly
State Pepper: Jalapeno

VI. SCRIPTURES from the BIBLE

EXODUS 3:4

And when the Lord saw that he turned aside to see, God called unto him out of the midst of the bush, and said, Moses, Moses. And he said, Here am I.

CHAPTER 14

VIRGINIA

"MY" Signature Virginia 'Gospel Bird' (Fried Chicken) and Accompaniments Menu

-HIGHLIGHTS-

I. MENU

"MY" Signature Virginia 'Gospel Bird' (Fried Chicken)
Virginia Dipping Sauce
Virginia Greens
Cornmeal Muffins
Blueberry Cobbler
Virginia Iced Tea

II. RECIPES

"MY" Signature Virginia 'Gospel Bird' (Fried Chicken) Recipe

Amount	Ingredients
2 ½ pounds	fryer, cut-up
2 teaspoons	Kosher salt
1 teaspoon	black pepper
½ teaspoon	red pepper
2 cups	all purpose flour
1 cup	corn meal
2 cups	vegetable oil

Directions

1. Wash chicken and pat dry. Set aside.
2. In a plastic bag, combine seasonings, all purpose flour and corn meal.
3. Coat each piece of chicken with flour mixture.
4. Heat oil to 350 degrees F.
5. Fry chicken until golden brown

"Virginia" Dipping Sauce

Amount	Ingredients
1 cup	pineapple juice
½ cup	brown sugar
½ teaspoon	cayenne pepper
1 teaspoon	chili pepper
½ teaspoon	salt

Directions

1. Place all ingredients in a medium saucepan and cook on low for 15 minutes stirring constantly.

ACCOMPANIMENTS

"Virginia" Greens

Amount	Ingredients
1	Virginia ham bone, cured
3 quarts	water
2 bunches	collard greens, picked, cut and washed

1 pound	dandelion greens, cleaned and picked
1 pound	kale, washed, and cut-up
1 tablespoon	salt
1 tablespoon	sugar
½ tablespoon	red pepper flakes
2 tablespoons	lard

Directions

1. In a large stockpot, boil ham bone in water for 40 minutes.
2. Stir in all of the prepared greens. Cover and cook for 30 minutes.
3. Stir well and add remaining ingredients. Cover and cook for 45 additional minutes.

Corn Bread Muffins

Amount	Ingredients
2 ½ cups	white coarsely ground meal
½ cup	flour
1 tablespoon	baking soda
½ teaspoon	baking powder
2 tablespoons	sugar
2 cups	buttermilk
3	eggs, whipped
2 tablespoons	lard

Directions

1. Preheat oven to 400 degrees F. Prepare muffin pan. Set aside.
2. In a large bowl, sift all dry ingredients together.
3. Combine liquid ingredients. Stir into dry ingredients.
4. Pour into prepared muffin pan and bake until golden brown.

"MY" Virginia Blueberry Cobbler

Amount	Ingredients
2 ½ cups	all-purpose flour
1 ½ cups	sugar
1 ½ cups	butter
2	eggs, beaten
3 cups	blueberries, fresh
1 teaspoon	lemon juice
½ teaspoon	cinnamon
¼ cup	all-purpose flour
1 1/ 2 cups	sugar

Directions

1. In a food processor, combine flour sugar, butter and eggs. Make into a dough.
2. Divide and roll out into 2 -13 x 9x 2-inch size doughs.
3. Place one dough into bottom of pan and prick. Bake at 400degrrees F for 5 minutes and cool down.
4. In a large bowl, combine blueberries, lemon juice cinnamon, all-purpose flour and sugar.
5. Stir well.
6. Pour blueberry mixture on top of partially baked crust.
7. Top with second crust and prick top and bake for 50 minutes at 350 degrees F.

"MY" Virginia Sweet Red Tea

Amount	Ingredients
2 gallons	water
5 bags	red tea bags
2 cups	sugar
1 quart	red cherry juice

Directions

1. Boil water. Steep tea.
2. Add sugar red cherry juice.

III. GOSPEL MUSIC ND MUSICIANS

NOT KNOWN

IV. WORSHIP ON THE PLANTATION

Slave Worshipping

"Pattyroller is a gang of white men gitting together goin' through de country catching an beatin' 'em up if dey had no remit. Marster's slaves met an' worshipped from house to house, an honey, we talked to My God all us wanted."

Ex-Slave Crawley

Interesting Note

Virginia Invention

"My master tole us de nigger started the railroad. An' sat a nigger lookin' at a boilin'coffee pot on a stovr onr day got the idea that he could cause it to run by putting wheels on it.

Dis nigger being a blackamith put his thpughts into action by makin. Wheels coffee pot on it, an' by some kinder manner he made it run, an' the by some kinder means he made it run an' the idea wuz stole from him an' dey built de steam engine."

Ex-Slave John Berry

-Oldest Black Baptist Church in Virginia-

The oldest Black Church in Virginia is First African Baptist Church in Petersburg, Virginia.

The church was started in 1756.

V. STATE FACTS

VIRGINIA

Virginia entered the Union in: June 25, 1788
Slave State 1788-1865 =77 years
Origin of the Name: Virginia was named for Queen Elizabeth I of England

State Nickname: Old Dominium
State Motto: "Sic Semper Tyrannis"

(Thus Always to Tyrants)]

State Song: "Carry Me Back To Old Virginia"

Number of Counties: 95 counties

Bordering States: Kentucky, Maryland,
North Carolina, Tennessee, West Virginia and, Washington, DC
State Capital: Richmond
Largest City: Richmond

Presidential Birthplace:
Georga Washington
Thomas Jefferson
James Madison
William Henry Harrisaon

John Tyler
Zzchary Tayloe
Woodrow Wilson

State Bird: Cardinal

State Dog: American fox hound
State Insect: Tiger Swallowtail butterfly

State Fish: Brook Trout

State Shell: Oyster
State Flower: American dogwood
State Tree: American dogwood

State Beverage: Milk

State Dance: Square Dance

VI. SCRIPTURES from the BIBLE

MATTHEW 28:19,20

19 Go ye therefore, and teach all nations, baptizing them in the name of the FATHER, and of the Son, and of the Holy Ghost.

20 Teaching them to observe all things whatsoever I have commanded you: and lo I am with you always even to the end of the world. Amen.

CHAPTER 15

LIST OF AFRICAN COUNTRIES FROM WHICH SLAVE TRADES WERE MADE FROM 1619-?

WESTERN AFRICA

1. Benin- Porto-Novo
2. Burkina-Faso- Ouagadouhgoe
3. Cape Verde-Praia
4. Gambia -Banjul
5. Ghana -Accra
6. Guinea-Conakry
7. Guinea-Bissau -Bissau
8. Ivory Coast-Yamoussou Kio
9. Liberia- Monrovia
10. Mali- Bamako
11. Mauretania – Noaakchott
12. Niger -Niamey
13. Nigeria-Abuja
14. Senegal - Dakar
15. Sierra Leone – Freetown
16. Togo- Lome

SOUTHERN AFRICA

1. Angola -Luande
2. Botswana-Gaborone
3. Burundi -Bujumbura
4. Democratic Republic of the Congo -Kinshasha
5. Equatorial Guinea -Malabo
6. Gabon -Libreville
7. Kenya-Nairobi
8. Lesotho-Maseru

9. Madagascar- Antananarivo
10. Malawi- Lilongwe
11. Mozambique Maputo
12. Namibia- Windhoek
13. Republic of the Congo-Brazzaville
14. Rwanda - Kigali
15. Swaziland- Mbabane
16. Tanzania Dares Salaam
17. Uganda Kampala
18. Zambia Lusaka
19. Zimbabwe Harare

EASTERN AFRICA

1. Comoros-Moroni
2. Eriterea -Asmara
3. Ethiopia-Addis Adaba
4. Djibouti -Djibouti
5. Ychelles -Victoria
6. Reunion -Saint -Denis
7. Mayotte - Mamoudzou
8. South Sudan -Juba
9. Uganda - Kampala
10. Rwanda - Kigalia

NORTHERN AFRICA

1. Egypt- Cairo
2. Libya -Tripoli
3. Mauritania -Nouakehoft
4. Morocco -Rabat
5. Sudan – Khartoum
6. South Sudan- Juba

7. Tunisia -Tunis
8. West Sahara - Laayoune

CENTRAL AFRICAN COUNTRIES

1. Angola -Luande
2. Cameroom Yaounde
3. Chad – N'Djamena
4. The Central African Republic – Bangue
5. Republic of the Congo -Brazzaville
6. Equatorial Guinea – Malabo
7. Sao Tome & Principe – Sao Tome

SCRIPTURE:

GENESIS 1;1
1 In the beginning God created the heaven and the earth.

CHAPTER 16

BLACK INVENTORS AND THEIR INVENTIONS

INVENTIONS		INVENTORS
1.	Paper	Africans
2.	Chess	Africans
3.	Alphabet	Africans
4.	Medicine	Africans
5.	Civilization	Africans
6.	Aeroplane Propelling	Jane S. Adams
7.	Biscuit Cutter	A.P. Asbourne
8.	Folding Bed	L.C. Bailey
9.	Corn Changer	J. A. Bauer
10.	Rotary Engine	Andrew J. Beard
11.	Car Coupler	Andrew J. Beard
12.	Letter Box	G.E. Becket
13.	Stainless Steel Pads	Alfred Benjamin
14.	Corn Planter	Henry Blair
15.	Cotton Planter	Henry Blair
16.	Ironing Board	Sarah Boone
17.	Pace Maker Controls	Otis Boykins
18.	Guided Missile	Otis Boykins
19.	Torpedo Discharger	H. Bradberry
20.	Street Sweeper	Charles Brooks
21.	Disposable Syringe	Phil Brooks
22.	Horse Bride Bit	L.F. Brown
23.	Home Security System	Marie Brown
24.	Horseshoe	Oscar E. Brown
25.	Lawn Mower	John A. Burr
26.	Typewriter	Burridge & Marshman

27.	Train Alarm	R. A. Butler
28.	Image Converter	Geo. Carruthers
29.	FOR Radiation Detector	Geo. Carruthers
30.	Peanut Butter	Geo. W. Carver
31.	Paints and Stains	Geo. W. Carver
32.	Lotions and Soaps	Geo. W. Carver
33.	Pillow Utilizing Air/Water	Larry L. Christie
34.	Track Athlete Trainer	John Clarke
35.	Automatic Fishing Reel	George Cook
36.	Ice Cream Mold	A.L. Cralle
37.	Horse Riding Saddle	Wm. D. Davis
38.	Shoe	W.A. Deitz
39.	Player Piano	Joseph Dickinson
40.	Arm for Record Player	Joseph Dickinson
41.	Door Stop	O. Dorsey
42.	Door Knob	O. Dorsey
43.	Photo Print Wash	Clstonis J. Dorticus
44.	Photo Embossing	Clatonia J. Dorticus
45.	Postal Letter Box	P.B. Downing
46.	Blood Plasma	Dr. Charles Drew
47.	Toilet (Commode)	T. Elkins
48.	Furniture Caster	David A. Fisher
49.	Guitar	Robert Flemming, Jr.
50.	IKenga-Gyroplane	David Gittens
51.	Ikenga/MKS-Automobile	David Gittens
52.	Skooterboard	David Gittens
53.	Golf Tee	George F. Grant
54.	Motor	J. Gregory
55.	Lantern	Michael Harney
56.	Thermo Hair Curlers	Solomon Harper
57.	Space Shuttle Retrieval Arm	W.M. Harwell

58.	Ice Cream	Augusta Jackson
59.	Gas Burner	B.F. Jackson
60.	Kitchen Table	H.A. Jackson
61.	Programable Remote Control	Joseph N. Jackson
62.	Video Commander	Joseph N. Jackson
63.	O.F. Cable/NonMwr Sheath	Artis Jenkins
64.	Bicycle Frame	Isaac R. Johnson
65.	Sani Phone	Jerry Johnson
66.	Wrench	John A. Johnson
67.	Super Soaker	Lonnie Johnson
68.	Eye Protector	P. Johnson
69.	Egg Beater	W. Johnson
70.	Defroster	Frederick M. Jones
71.	Air Conditioning Unit	Frederick M. Jones
72.	Two-Cycle Gas Engine	Frederick M. Jones
73.	Internal Combustion Engine	Frederick M. Jones
74.	Starter Generator	Frederick M. Jones
75.	Refrigerator Controls	Frederick M. Jones
76.	Bottle Caps	Jones & Long
77.	Clothes Dryer	John H. Jordan
78.	Electric Lamp	Latimer & Nichels
79.	Printing Press	W.A. Lavalette
80.	Laser Fuels	Lester Lee
81.	Pressure Cooker	Maurice W. Lee
82.	Envelope Seal	F.S. Lester
83.	Window Cleaner	A.L. Lewis
84.	Pencil Sharper	John L. Love
85.	Fire Extinguisher	Tom J. Marshel
86.	Lock	W.A. Martin
87.	Shoe Lasting Machine	Jan Matzeliger
88.	Lubricators	Elijah McCoy

89.	Rocket Catapult	Hugh MacDonald
90.	Elevator	Alexander Miles
91.	Gas Mask	Garrett Morgan
92.	Traffic Signal	Garrett Morgan
93.	Hair Brush	Lyda Newman
94.	Heating Furnace	Alice A. Parker
95.	Air Ship (Blimp)	J. F. Pickering
96.	Folding Chair	Purdy J. Sadgwar
97.	Hand Stamp	W.B. Purvis
98.	Fountain Pen	W.B. Purvis
99.	Dust Pan	L.P. Ray
100.	Insect Destroyer Gun	A.C. Richardson
101.	Baby Buggy	W.H. Richardson
102.	Sugar Refinement	N. Rillieux
103.	Pressing Comb	Walter Sammons
104.	Hair Dressing Device	Walter Sammons
105.	Clothes Drier	G.T. Sampson
106.	Cellular Phone	Henry Sampson
107.	Urinalysis Machine	Dewey Sanderson
108.	Hydraulic Shock Absorber	Ralph Sanderson
109.	Curtain Rod	S.R. Scottron
110.	Multi Stage Rocket	Adolph Shams
111.	Lawn Sprinkler	J.W. Smith
112.	Automatic Gear Shift	R.B. Spikes
113.	Refrigerator	J. Standard
114.	Mop	T.W. Steward
115.	Cattle Roping Apparatus	Darryl Thomas
116.	Stairclimbing Wheel Chair	Rufus J. Weaver
117.	Polym. Water Reduc. Paint-	Morris B. Williams
118.	Helicopter	Paul E. Williams
119.	Fire Escape Ladder	J. B. Winters

SHARON HUNT

120.	Telephone Transmitter	Granville T. Woods
121.	Electric Cut Off Switch	Granville T. Woods
122.	Relay Instrument	Granville T. Woods
123.	Telephone System	Granville T. Woods
124.	Electro Mech Brake	Granville T. Woods
125.	Galvanic Battery	Granville T. Woods
126.	Electric Railway System	Granville T. Woods
127.	Roller Coaster	Granville T. Woods
128.	Aerto Air Brake	Granville T. Woods

Source: The Black Inventions Museum- A Non-Profit Corporation Los Angeles, Calif. 90076

REFERENCES

1. The Holy Bible, King James Version, Broadman & Holman Publishers. Nashville, Tennessee, 1996.
2. Johnson, James Weldon and J. Rosamond Johnson: The Book of American Negro Spirituals. Viking Press, 1962.
3. Slave Narratives, WPA 1936-1938, Library of Congress, Washington, D.C.
4. Woodson, Carter G.: The Story of the Negro Retold. The Associated Publishers, Inc. Washington, D.C.

SCRIPTURE from the BIBLE:

PROVERBS 29:18

Where there is no vision, the people perish: but he that keepth the law, happy is he.

CPSIA information can be obtained
at www.ICGtesting.com
Printed in the USA
BVHW031948240319
543549BV00001B/33/P